JOHN TIECH | JOHN ISAACS

Unlearning & Relearning

A GUIDE TO COLLEGE COMPOSITION

Kendall Hunt
publishing company

Cover image © Shutterstock, Inc.

Kendall Hunt
p u b l i s h i n g   c o m p a n y
www.kendallhunt.com
Send all inquiries to:
4050 Westmark Drive
Dubuque, IA 52004-1840

for Angela, JT, and ART
and
for Beth, who said yes

Contents

Chapter [1]

Beginnings

What do the following statements have in common?

1. Never question authority.

2. Don't ask for more. Be content with what you have.

3. Work hard to blend in with others.

4. In order to stay out of trouble, don't take sides.

5. Before you proceed, read the instructions.

Give up? Well, don't. Give it another five minutes.

In this chapter about beginnings, the opening words of the first chapter, the beginning of this book of English composition, the focus now, and throughout the textbook, is *you* and *your* beginning: what you learned up to this point, where you will go, and what you will unlearn and relearn in order to become a more confident, fair writer and thinker.

Look again at the opening five statements. You may have noticed that they are all imperative sentences conveying advice, a command, and a request. You may even describe the tone of some of the statements as that of forbiddance. Each statement also has something else in common. You may have heard and obeyed these commands from the onset, from your beginnings, from those who love you, those who instructed you in order to protect you. These statements or commands may still be engrained in your mind and may dictate how you act or respond. You may not even be aware to what extent these learned statements dictate how you think, act, and respond.

You may be asking yourself, "So what's the big deal?" Well, if you believe these statements unequivocally, without question, then you are not thinking about exceptions, about other points of view and other possibilities that may expedite your success in many areas, including writing and thinking. You must first be aware of what you need to overcome, what the weaknesses in your thinking processes are, before you can unlearn, reconsider, and relearn. An anonymous quip (although sometimes accredited to humorists from Mark Twain to Josh Billings and Artemus Ward), in part, applies here: "It ain't what you don't know that gets you in trouble. It's what you know for sure that just ain't so." If you stubbornly hold onto views that are half-truths or downright wrong, then you may likely find yourself in trouble, or perhaps even worse, in a state of ignorant bliss. "What you don't know" or do not even consider *can* severely hamper your thinking and progress and probably factors into how people judge or regard you.

Look again at the opening five statements. Surely, progress has been made by questioning authority. Scientific breakthroughs often begin with questions about what is accepted as true, resulting in new theories and major shifts of thinking. Slavery was abolished and women achieved the right to vote due to rebellion against smothering authority. Genocide proceeded due to unquestioned obedience to authority. Somewhere along the line, you may have understood that you had to unlearn "never question authority" because you had learned to think for yourself and formulate your own ideas and opinions instead of blindly following those of others.

Consider now the second imperative statement. It is admirable at times to be content with what you have. However, if you are stuck in that mindset, will you ever try to achieve more? Does content necessarily mean exultant or joyful?

Have you ever questioned any of the last three opening statements? Why must you always blend in? Don't you want to stand out, be different, and be seen and heard? Why should you keep your opinions to yourself and not take sides or a stance, especially about something you greatly believe in? How might smothering your point of view hinder you? Finally, might you learn and remember more by trying to figure something out by yourself instead of waiting for instructions or following someone else's instructions?

Hopefully, by now, you can answer the opening chapter question. All five imperative statements are what you may have learned and what you must unlearn and reconsider in order to think for yourself. Unlearning is often difficult. Someone may have told you, a long time ago, that Santa does not slide down the chimney with a sack of presents and that a parent, not the Tooth Fairy, slipped a few dollars under your pillow when you lost a tooth. At this point in your life, however, it is time to figure out things for yourself by seeking and considering points of view other than your own.

It is time to unlearn and relearn many "rules" about writing before you can take control and find your own distinctive literary voice. For example, you may have learned never to use the pronoun "I" when you write. It is time to unlearn that. There are certainly many occasions when the first perspective is called for, even encouraged. You may also think that you need a concluding summation sentence in every paragraph, or that criticism and argumentation are negative exercises that won't get you anywhere.

What may have been forgotten or lost throughout your many years of English classes is *you—your* voice, *your* perspective, *your* style. You may have been asked to synthesize the work of others for so long that you have lost yourself and your purpose in writing certain assignments. You may not have had grammar instruction since grade school and may believe that correct grammar does not matter when, in fact, it does. People will judge you for your lapses in grammar. You may have been so restricted by rigid outlines or a prescribed

structure that you have forgotten what it is like to be free to explore your own style, word choice, and topic. Perhaps, if you consider writing a chore, you have felt that little is at stake for you when you read, synthesize, or create.

The assignments in this textbook are "you" centered in order to help you unlearn in order to reclaim your narrative voice. You may not have written much lately about what matters to you, and that includes writing about yourself and topics you find fascinating or urgent.

Many of the essays included in this textbook were written by first-year university students who not only found their voices but also a receptive audience eager to discuss the points raised in the essays. Some of the essays are first drafts and works in progress, shared by first-year students who fine-tuned their essays after peer criticism. Many of these students heard their words read and discussed in a class workshop setting for the very first time. Immediate peer feedback helped them to comprehend the impact, or lack of impact, of their words. The same opportunity is here for you. You have an audience, one you can learn from and one that can learn something from you. Perhaps you can even make them *feel* something. How might that make you feel?

The beginning of an essay should engage the reader at once. This chapter began with the purpose of getting your attention right away to make you think—a way to engage an audience from the onset. You were asked what the five statements had in common. Now, take a look at your peers in your composition class. How will you engage them and make them think? What might you have in common? What is on your minds? What do you want to talk about, address, debate, or build?

And so we begin. Here is your opportunity, a new beginning, to be heard, seen, and considered. Listen to other voices. Unlearn what does not make sense. Listen to what does. Allow yourself to learn and relearn. Build your narrative voice with logic, authority, and urgency.

So let's begin. It is time to turn the page.

Chapter [2]

The Diagnostic

© Syda Productions/Shutterstock.com

Unlearning

The word "diagnostic" may have a negative connotation for you. You may think of the word "diagnosis," an act or examination performed by a medical professional to identify, or ascertain, the nature of an illness. You may also think of tests performed by a mechanic on your engine or carburetor to diagnose why your car will not start.

Relearning

A diagnostic essay for English composition, written at the beginning of a semester, is not a test. However, it is an examination of sorts. Your teacher, your peers, and, most importantly, you will examine your essay in order to see where you are right now as a reader and writer—as a student responding to a prompt. You may also read and respond to the responses of other students in your class to evaluate their current strengths and weaknesses.

What is the purpose of writing a diagnostic, as well as reading some of your peers' responses? First, almost immediately, you will realize that when you write, you have an audience. Your audience for this composition class will include your peers: a group of students, like you, who will be placed in a workshop setting, perhaps sitting in desks arranged in a circle, facing each other and responding, in a constructive and kind way, to the strengths and weaknesses of the essay placed before them. Right away, you will learn that you are not alone. You are a *student*—an observer, participator, and learner among other students who may receive similar responses or diagnoses from the critical readers of your essay. You may find comfort in knowing that the cause or nature of the weaknesses in your writing may not be entirely your fault, or not your fault at all. Instead, these flaws may be due to the lack of attention and focus on your own thoughts and positions over the past several years.

For example, even if you were not recommended to take advanced or AP English courses in high school, perhaps many of your assignments were aimed at synthesizing the written works of others or, in other words, using published sources to respond to a given prompt. A typical high school beginning semester project prompt may read like this: "Begin your research project by using index cards to document possible usable sources to show, through Biblical allegorical characterization and metaphorical transformations, the repercussions of lost innocence in John Knowles *A Separate Peace* and William Golding's *The Lord of the Flies*." The middle and ending class assignments may have been, for you, drearily similar.

Synthesizing activities have many benefits. You learn how to formulate a thesis. You plan how to use and organize your source material. You find ways to integrate some of your own material, including transitions. You become savvy at documenting and revising.

The problem becomes that, when relying so heavily on the words of others, paraphrasing closely and quoting directly, you find yourself more adept at copying and pasting than expressing, discovering, critiquing, or arguing. Your sources have so eloquently done so for you.

The second purpose of the diagnostic is to reveal what is at stake for you every time you choose a word, organize your thoughts, and build a sequence of sentences. You may not be graded for writing this diagnostic. However, each time you speak and write, people judge or evaluate you. Each time you share your thoughts, something is at stake for you. That is what you may have forgotten when you were repeatedly asked to synthesize the work of others. You may have forgotten yourself—*your* purpose, *your* voice.

The purpose of this diagnostic is to demonstrate that you are not alone, to begin to listen to, and appraise, your narrative voice, and to start a conversation, quite simply, about what makes writing good.

Let's start.

The Diagnostic Prompt

You may be wondering, right now, what you are doing here: at a college that may be far away from home; at a college that may not have been your first choice; in a core English composition class that you must take; in a chair next to a boy who is smiling and seems genuinely happy and eager to get started. You are not so eager. Perhaps you are not an English major, and you believe you have the basic reading and writing tools to get by not only in your major, but in life.

You tell yourself to keep an open mind. By the end of the class, however, the happy, eager boy has responded twelve times to your zero. You can already tell that your instructor has developed a rapport with certain students, and you are not one of them. Later, your roommate, whom you have known since your first year of high school, tells you she had a similar experience in her English class.

"Answer me this," she asks you. "Aren't there other courses that are more important and should be mandatory for all students instead of English composition courses? I know there are. What courses should replace composition? Like you, I had four years of English, even honors and AP English, and we got by just fine. So why do colleges force us to take this stuff all over again?"

In a few paragraphs, respond to your friend as best as you can. Draw upon your personal observations and experiences to come up with as thoughtful and complete of an argument as possible at this moment. Remember, you are responding to your friend, and you should not feel as if you are being tested or forced to come up with a singular or expected answer. Do your best to reflect upon your friend's question and render a genuine, contemplative reply.

college is a fresh start, where the work really matters. I feel like we have to go back to the basics to understand more intense courses.

Diagnostic Responses A, B, and C

Here are three responses to the diagnostic prompt. As you read the essays, think about which response is the best, and why. Support your critique with evidence, or textual support, from the essays. What makes one essay better than another? What has one student done well in one essay that the others failed to do? What has each writer, individually, done well? How can each writer do better? How would you describe the narrative voice you hear?

Also, as you consider each response, reflect upon the following strategies writers sometimes use in order to avoid the tougher work of responding to a prompt directly and thinking for themselves: using clichés; writing for the teacher; saying what's obvious or already known; or saying virtually nothing new or insightful at all. These are practices you need to *unlearn*. What you may need to *relearn* is to ask yourself some questions before you begin your response, and also throughout your essay. Who is my audience, and am I considering that audience in my response? What is my purpose, and what is at stake for me and perhaps for others in my writing? Is there evidence that my mind is moving throughout my response, or am I just marking time?

So what is working in the following diagnostics, what is not working, and why?

RESPONSE A

The masses need to heed this: today we must all work together to perform all kinds of tasks that must be done to avoid disaster and promote diversity. All individuals, wherever their ethnicity, must do their part to fill roles that others may not be able to fill. The obligation for sharing tasks and talents is a universal obligation. Unless we work together and open our minds, we will not be able to surmount certain obstacles. People must work together. Everyone has a niche. Some people are good with their hands. Some are good with their minds. When people of all races and genders put their hands and minds together, we can get things accomplished. Everyone, no matter where they live or what they do, can make a contribution. Sometimes making a contribution means doing things we do not want to do, or are forced to do. We are all faced with things we may not want to do, but do them anyway, since people by nature are pleasant and want to get along. That's why I think sociology classes should be mandatory. But it doesn't hurt to take English again. If we do not honor our responsibilities in literacy, writing, and communication, the world as we know it could crumble.

Think of the first year composition class as a type of melting pot. Students from all over the country (from the deep South to the far North, or from the east coast to the west or students raised on farms or in urban apartments, and students whose beliefs are rooted in one faith or another) find themselves in a room full of strangers and learn how to communicate and get along with one another. If, as a nation of divided immigrants, we, as a country, had not been forced to come together and work together in times of need, what would the consequences be? We would not have hospitals or paved roads. We would not have movie theaters. We would not have a system of taxation or representation to pay for things that we like or leaders who help us think. English classes that we are forced to take are one of the many things we are forced to do for the better sake of humanity. Would you rather be alone in dark, lonely hole, playing video games, or in a brightly lit classroom sharing ideas with others?

Everything hinges on forced learning. You are breaking the law as a parent if you do not force your child to go to school. Compulsory education is education by force. Force can be good. In some cultures, marriages are arranged and forced, and they turn out fine and at divorce rates lower than those who choose on their own to marry. Of course, you may not be forced to go to college, but if you do go, you are forced to do many things for your betterment, such as learning how to pay off loans, get along with a cranky or addicted roommate, and taking mandatory classes.

In conclusion, although taking sociology might help us all understand each other better, taking a mandatory English class or two for all incoming college students, no matter of their ethnicity or experience, will help since so much hinges on it. Until you learn to be flexible and work with others, you will not succeed. And nowhere is this more apparent than a first year composition class.

✈ RESPONSE B

Someone important once said that you should only read what you want to read. A book that you are forced to read really won't have much of an impact on you. Throughout high school, I agreed with this point of view. Sometimes I don't like the way an author writes, with too much setting or flowery atmosphere in the beginning and no action. With <u>Moby Dick,</u> I wasn't about to read the small print and the seemingly endless number of pages. So, in high school, I read SparkNotes and became proficient in rearranging words and finding synonyms.

I didn't read Hemingway's <u>The Old Man and the Sea</u>, nor Steinbeck's <u>The Grapes of Wrath,</u> nor Ayn Rand's <u>The Fountainhead</u>. But during summer break, when I was bored, I picked up <u>The Fountainhead</u> and began to read it. In high school, I didn't like the idea the binding was so tight so that I had to pull the pages apart to read the last words of the left page lines and the front words of the right page lines. During the summer, however, that did not seem to matter as I began to read. Pulling back the pages seemed effortless and I could not stop reading. Howard Rourke's devotion to architecture brought warm tears to my eyes—it would you too! If you read it, I'm sure you know what I'm talking about. It's a great book.

Rourke's devotion to building was amazing. In high school, while other students who were forced to read the book and actually read it were talking about how great it was, I was left out. I just didn't know how a novel could immerse me into another, new world, a world I would probably never be able to know about otherwise unless I read about it.

Writing, on the other hand, is just the opposite of reading, but without writers there would be nothing to read. The two are dependent on each other and often they are inter-interdependent. The Wolf of Wall Street is modern The Great Gatsby. If there had never been The Great Gatsby, there never would have been The Wolf of Wall Street.

So English courses should remain mandatory because reading and writing must be done to cultivate communication management and open our minds and inspire us. Certainly one can communicate via the phone, but not as efficiently to large numbers. Form letters cannot be read to one by secretaries over the phone. It would be inefficient. If it was decreed that members of Congress must speak to all constituents one-on-one to reassess what needed to be done in Washington, nothing would be accomplished. Instead, surveys are forwarded to constituents.

We make up excuses for doing required work, but seldom do these excuses justify avoiding the required work, and we miss out on things that we may not otherwise come to know.

RESPONSE C

I feel you, man. I like to work with my hands and build things. I'm a carpenter. Make us take up a trade and force me to take a trade class. I never took honors or AP English and I have a hard time getting things from my head to the paper just like we all does. I'd rather just tell you straight out something than put it down and then has you read it. Why waste the time? But these teacher I had for four years keep drilling the idea that writing things down makes it all better. I can tell you it doesn't make my wrist feel better. I don't mind reading short things like comic book or sports blogs or even subtitles on films not made in the good old USA. When my mom told me to watch a Persian film with her, I didn't even know what that meant. Only thing Persian I hear of was a rug. I said no I would not like it. She put in on anyway. For some reason, I stuck around and I started to read the subtitles and I got to liking it. It was about a boy who lost his sisters shoes, and how they made a plan to share his shoes so they would not get in trouble with their parents. They lived in Iran, wherever that was, or is. I look on a map to see where that was, and it took me a while to find it. But then I put it out of my mind for a while. I figured it had nothing to do with me, and never would, this place so far away. But then my teacher have this extra credit project she pushed about how people are people, which I didn't want to write about. But then I did, because I was reminded of that movie I watched, or actually, watched and read, and I thought that maybe I did want to say something about it. But then I stopped, and figured other people could write it better, or you could already find an essay from a good writer who had already written it. So whats the use? But then I started to write and I kept writing about how these two kids lived in a different time and culture and had different problems then what I am and had different food and drink, but what was expected of them and what drove them were things that were the same with me and my sister. It was if they weren't that different. But then I stopped there and let it go. My teacher say I was onto something important and wants me to go on with it. I don't know. Teacher says I do. Maybe it has something to do with another kind of building, like building things like words on paper. But who knows. I sure don't, do I?

Class Exercise: In-Class Debate and Discussion

1. What do you expect in an introduction and conclusion? Which student has the best opening line? Why is it the best? Which student has the weakest conclusion? Why is it weak?

2. Which student considers audience best? Use textual evidence to support your claim.

3. Which student answers the question most directly? Who has the most to say, or, for you, has the most impact? Do any of the students get off track or lose focus? If so, where?

4. Which student has the best command of language? Who has the best command of sentence structure? In which essay(s) do a lack of language skills and sentence structure disrupt the narrative flow and your concentration?

5. In your estimation, which student's words are most meaningful for both self and audience? How can you tell?

6. Circle the clichés and generalizations that you hear. Is there a correlation between the number of clichés and generalizations in a given essay and how interesting or significant the essay is to you? Besides generalizations, are you familiar with, or can you identify, any other flaws in logic in the essays?

7. Do any of the essays include statements that do not make sense or are confusing? If so, where?

8. Which student do you believe is thinking the most when answering the questions? Provide evidence for your assessment. What student do you believe is thinking the least? How can you tell?

9. Examine the content, or *what* is said. Now examine the narrative voice, or *how* the content is delivered (what you hear). Do you hear different voices within an individual essay? Locate the different voices you hear. How would you describe these voices? Do the different voices add to or distract from the essay's content?

10. Without looking back, what line or lines do you remember? Why do you think these lines are memorable? What parts of the essays did you forget, or do you find not meaningful for you or for the writer? Why?

11. Which essay is most believable, authentic, or genuine? How do both the content (the *what*) and the narrative voice (the *how*) contribute to the authenticity?

12. Based on the essays you have just read, what do you believe that you and your peers should strive to unlearn? What would you like to relearn that you have forgotten?

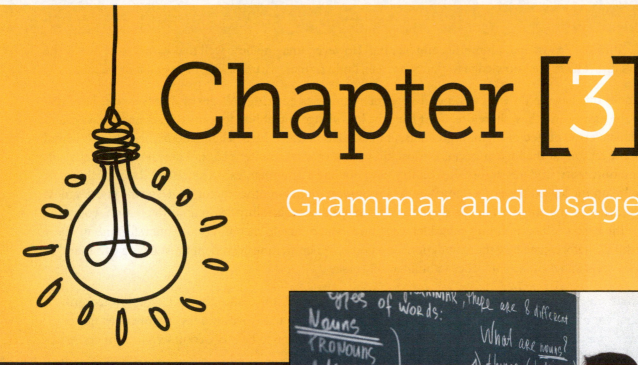

Chapter [3]

Grammar and Usage

© Undrey/Shutterstock.com

Unlearning

1. Me and my twin sister don't have the same hobbies and interests.

2. One of the boys left their cellphone on the bleacher.

3. The team will play their final game on Sunday.

4. Otto worked relentless until the entire interior of the house was painted.

5. Running toward the mountain, the cliffs appeared rugged and impassable.

You will have the opportunity at the end of this chapter to address the grammar and sentence structure problems in the above sentences, errors commonly found in student writing. First, consider this opportunity to refresh your knowledge of the parts of speech.

Relearning

Building a house is a complicated process that involves many steps, and each step has its own beginning, middle, and end. When building a house, builders always begin from the bottom-up, starting with the foundation. Next, they frame the house and eventually put up walls and a roof, and finally, the builders get to the specifics such as wiring, plumbing, and heating. However, imagine how well that would work out if the builders didn't have the knowledge to pour concrete, build frames, wire a house, or install a furnace?

What does this have to do with writing? Today, many students entering colleges and universities have forgotten the basics, and they, therefore, don't have the knowledge and ability to write the advanced essays and research papers expected of them. A great disconnect exists between high school and higher education, and part of the reason for that disconnect is the lost knowledge of what a sentence is and how it works. Many college and university students across the country have not had a grammar lesson since eighth or ninth grade. Not only can the lapsed time be a culprit in the lost information, but other factors, such as the effectiveness of the teacher or the attention of the student, may also bear responsibility. No matter the reason, you must relearn the basics. When building, a builder must understand how to mix and pour concrete, among many other things, before installing the foundation for a house. When writing, a student must have a command of sentence parts and structure in order to build a solid essay.

Grammar can be difficult to teach and learn. In fact, colleges and universities have classes devoted only to grammar for an entire semester, but in a college composition course, that amount of time does not exist. However, grammar matters, and brief refresher lessons will help you to be more confident in your construction of a well-planned essay.

Why does grammar matter? When you misspeak, often the person listening to you is silently correcting your grammar instead of listening to what you say. The same is true when you write. If your readers are interrupted by repeated flaws in grammar, they may just stop reading. They may quickly judge you and dismiss the potential value of what you have to say because of your inability to clearly say it. Errors in grammar and sentence construction often cause problems with clarity. Such errors may diminish your authority and credibility. For example, look at the following sentences found in student essays.

1. I was bored so I said, "I want to bake Grandma!"

2. My two favorite hobbies are throwing darts and poodles.

3. I told my english teacher, "Your the best teacher their ever was."

Hopefully, you see the problems with the first two sentences. What's the different in meaning between "I want to bake, Grandma!" and "I want to bake Grandma!" In the "two favorite hobbies" sentence, the writer fails to include an important word in the chain of thought: My two favorite hobbies are throwing darts and *raising* poodles. What is the irony in the third sentence?

A missing comma, an error in sentence construction, errors in grammar, and other problems with your essay's foundation can, as you see, weaken your credibility. Therefore, this is the perfect time to relearn the basics and start with the building blocks of essay construction.

Learning grammar as a three-step process can help you understand the makeup of a sentence and how it works. Much like building a house, the three-step process of grammar helps you build a sentence from the bottom-up, starting with the parts of speech, progressing to the sentence parts, and then building to clauses and sentence types.

You will use FIGURE 1 to help you with the three step process as you progress throughout this chapter.

STEP 1: Identify the Parts of Speech
[Articles, Nouns, Pronouns, Verbs, Adjectives, Adverbs, Conjunctions, Prepositions, Verbals (Gerund, Participle, Infinitive)]

The boy proudly gave Sally, a friend, the tiny bat and ball as her gift.

STEP 2: Identify the Sentence Parts
[Subjects, Verbs, Compliments (Direct Object, Indirect Object, Predicate Nominative, Predicate Adjective), Prepositional Phrases, Appositives or Appositive Phrases, and Verbal Phrases (Gerund Phrase, Participial Phrase, Infinitive Phrase)]

The boy proudly gave Sally, a friend, the tiny bat and ball as her gift.

STEP 3: Identify Clauses and Sentence Types
[Clauses (Independent, Dependent) & Sentence Types (Simple, Compound, Complex, Compound-Complex)]

The boy proudly gave Sally, a friend, the tiny bat and ball as her gift.

FIGURE 1: Grammar as a three-step process.

To briefly explain, you will completely identify all of the important grammatical aspects of a sentence using a three-step process, and you must follow the order of operations presented. In other words, you must complete step one entirely before moving on to step two, and you must complete step two before you complete step three. Also, within each step, there is a process to follow. Think of learning grammar as you would learn a simple math problem.

Step 1: Identifying the Parts of Speech

The parts of speech are the most basic, fundamental components of a sentence. The ability to identify each part of speech, as well as its function, will help you to build stronger sentences moving forward. Follow this order of operations:

1. Articles

2. Nouns

3. Pronouns

4. Verbs (Verbals if you have any)

5. Adjectives

6. Adverbs

7. Conjunctions

8. Prepositions

9. Interjections

Articles

In a sentence, articles ("a," "an," and "the") appear right before a noun or noun equivalent and function as adjectives. Why are articles adjectives? They modify nouns ("*a* toaster"; "*the* dog"). Since articles are easy to identify, you should easily be able to identify the nouns they modify. Refer back to your sample sentence. How many articles can you identify?

The boy proudly gave Sally, a friend, the tiny bat and ball as her gift.

The sample sentence has three articles. When you identify articles, you can label them as "art" for article or "adj" for adjective. The indefinite articles "a" and "an" modify a nonspecific noun, while the definite article "the" modifies a particular or specific noun. Furthermore, the article "a" is used only in front of nouns that begin with a consonant, while the article "an" is used only in front of nouns that begin with vowels or nouns that begin with vowel sounds. Use the marking that you think will work best for your identification purposes.

Art   Art   Art
The boy proudly gave Sally, a friend, the tiny bat and ball as her gift.

Nouns

In a sentence, a noun is the name of a person, place, thing, or an idea. Two different types of nouns exist: proper nouns and common nouns. Proper nouns are the names of a specific person, place, thing, or idea. Common nouns are the names of a general person, place, thing, or an idea. Notice that proper nouns are capitalized, unlike common nouns. The chart below provides examples of proper and common nouns.

	Person	Place	Thing
Proper Nouns	John Smith; Jane Smith; Mrs. Wilson; Mallory	Princeton University; Pittsburgh; Target; Lake Erie	Fido; Sadie; Hershey; Barbie; *Star Wars*; July 4, 1776
Common Nouns	boy; girl; teacher; student	university; city; store; lake	dog; cat; chocolate; toy; movie; date

Referring back to your sample sentence, how many nouns can you identify?

The boy proudly gave Sally, a friend, the tiny bat and ball as her gift.

The sample sentence has six nouns, and they are a mix of both the proper nouns and common nouns. Label the proper nouns with a capital "N" and the common nouns with a lower case "n."

 $\overset{n}{}$ $\overset{N}{}$ $\overset{n}{}$ $\overset{n}{}$ $\overset{n}{}$ $\overset{n}{}$
The <u>boy</u> proudly gave <u>Sally</u>, a <u>friend</u>, the tiny <u>bat</u> and <u>ball</u> as her <u>gift</u>.

Before moving on to the next part of speech, take a moment to think about all of the words that have been identified already. Take a look below.

Art n   N Art n   Art   n   n   n
The boy proudly gave Sally, a friend, the tiny bat and ball as her gift.

As you can see, only six words remain that need identified. Essentially, you are not only using an order of operations but you are also using a process of elimination to help you identify the parts of speech.

Practice

Directions: Identify the nouns in the following sentences.

1. Tom hit the ball.

2. My friend Jake went home.

3. On June 10, 2020, I went to the concert.

Pronouns

Next, identify any pronouns that may appear in the sentence. Pronouns function as noun substitutes. Several different types of pronouns exist.

Type	Examples
Demonstrative Pronouns (They refer back to certain individuals or things)	this, that, these, those
Indefinite Pronouns (They don't refer to a definite quantity, person, or thing)	all, another, any, anyone, anybody, anything, both, each, either, everybody, everyone, everything, few, fewer, less, little, more, most, many, much, neither, none, nobody, nothing, one, several, some, somebody, something
Interrogative Pronouns (They ask a question)	who, whom, whose, which, what, whatever, whichever, whoever
Relative Pronouns (They begin dependent clauses and connect them to independent clauses)	that, which, who, whom, whose, what, whatever , whatsoever, whichever, whoever, whosoever, whomever, whomsoever, whosesoever

The demonstrative, indefinite, interrogative, and relative pronouns are not the only types of pronouns you will encounter. The personal pronouns have been saved for last, and separated from the rest, because they will serve an important role moving forward.

First-person pronouns are listed below. For students, first-person pronouns are primarily used for reflective, narrative, or other personal writing, since they usually refer to "I" or "me."

First Person Pronouns	
Singular	I, me, my, mine, myself
Plural	we, us, our, ours, ourselves

Second-person pronouns are used intentionally in writing to talk directly to the reader. Therefore, the subject is most often about "you." Usually the "you" or second-person perspective is used when giving a set of instructions or directions. For students, second-person writing is primarily used in business or technical writing. The second-person pronouns are as follows:

Second Person Pronouns
you, your, yours, yourself

You will notice that the second-person pronouns are not separated into singular and plural. That is because the same words are used for both the singular and plural pronouns.

Finally, third-person pronouns refer to everyone else. Therefore, it is about "them." For students, third-person writing is primarily used in academic writing. Therefore, much of the work done in college will require third-person writing. The third-person pronouns are as follows:

Third Person Pronouns	
Singular	he, she, it, him, her, his, hers, its, himself, herself, itself
Plural	they, them, their, theirs, themselves

When you write, teachers will ask you to write in either a first-, second-, or third-person point-of-view. When you are given assignments that offer such instructions, referring back these personal pronouns will help you consider which point of view to use, and which is most appropriate for your essay.

Referring back to your sample sentence, how many pronouns can you identify?

The boy proudly gave Sally, a friend, the tiny bat and ball as her gift.

The sample sentence has one pronoun, and it is a third-person possessive pronoun. You may label this pronoun generally as "Pro" or specifically such as "3rd Per. Pro."

The boy proudly gave Sally, a friend, the tiny bat and ball as <u>her</u> gift.

Before moving on to the next part of speech, take a moment to think about all of the words that have been identified already. Take a look below.

Art n   N Art n   Art   n   n   Pro n
The boy proudly gave Sally, a friend, the tiny bat and ball as her gift.

As you can see, only five words remain that need identified, and you have looked only for the articles, nouns, and pronouns. If you are struggling with pronouns, you should practice identifying them before continuing to work on the process of identifying parts of speech. Remember, pronouns must agree in number and gender with their antecedents (the nouns they stand for or replace in the sentence).

Practice

Directions: Identify the pronouns in the following sentences.

1. He ate the salad while she ate the sandwich.

2. Melissa's dad took his medicine this morning.

3. My friend Jake went home.

4. On June 10, 2020, I went to the concert, and my mom was angry that I went.

Verbs (Predicates)

A verb is a word that represents action in a sentence, and it is the next part of speech you should identify in the process. It is also the last of the base components that you will have to follow in any type of specific order. Every sentence has a verb in it somewhere, and as you proceed to the sentence parts, clauses and sentence types later in this chapter, you will come to see why every sentence needs a verb. Additionally, verbs are also known as predicates, and this will be important to remember once you begin working with compliments in step two.

Even though there are three types of verbs, understand that only two of the three types are main verbs. Therefore, a sentence will have one of these two types of main verbs: action verbs and linking verbs.

Type	Examples
Action Verbs **(They show action in a sentence)**	writes, wrote, yells, yelled, visits, visited, sits, sat, plays, played, accepts, accepted, throws, threw, ran, run, makes, made
Linking Verbs **(They link two words together in a sentence)**	be, am, is, are, was, were, been, being, appear, become, grow, remain, feel, look, taste, seem, sound, smell, stay

When identifying verbs in a sentence, it is important to know whether they are action verbs or linking verbs, especially when moving on to the sentence parts. Knowing the type of verb will help you identify the type of compliment (object or predicate) you have in the sentence, if you even have any.

Sometimes, even the two main verbs need a little help, and that's where the helping verbs come to the rescue. Helping verbs are subordinate verbs that not only help the main verbs function properly, but they also need help from a main verb in order to survive. They are very dependent.

Helping Verbs
be, am, is, are, was, were, been, being, do, does, did, could, would, will, should, may, might, must, has, have, had, shall, ought

You may have noticed something interesting: there are many linking verbs and helping verbs that are the same. So, how can you tell the difference between the two when the "be" verbs can be either a linking verb or a helping verb? As a student, you must look at the functionality of the "be" verbs. You have to understand what a linking verb is doing and what a helping verb is doing. Take a look at the following examples:

EXAMPLE 1: Mary is happy.

EXAMPLE 2: Mary is working hard.

In the first example sentence, ask yourself how the verb "is" functions. The verb "is" links together "Mary" and "happy." In the second example sentence, how does "is" function? The verb "is" helps the action verb "working" operate correctly in the sentence. Think about it: the sentence would make no sense if it read "Mary working hard." In this case, the action verb "working" needs help.

Now look at the sample sentence for this chapter. How many verbs can you identify?

The boy proudly gave Sally, a friend, the tiny bat and ball as her gift.

The sample sentence has one verb, and it is the action verb "gave." Label an action verb by simply writing "AV" above it.

                          AV
The boy proudly <u>gave</u> Sally, a friend, the tiny bat and ball as her gift.

After looking for the articles, nouns, pronouns, and verbs, only four words are unidentified. Take a look below.

Art   n   AV   N Art n   Art   n   n   Pro n
The boy proudly gave Sally, a friend, the tiny bat and ball as her gift.

Practice

Directions: Identify the verbs in the following sentences.

1. He ate the salad while she ate the sandwich.

2. Tom hit the ball.

3. My friend Jake is happy.

4. You can come over and watch the movie.

5. He will be able to go to the concert

Adjectives

Since you have already identified the nouns, it only makes sense to proceed to the adjective, a part of speech that modifies or describes nouns. As mentioned earlier, nouns and adjectives work together, so you need to keep in mind that a sentence has to have a noun for any possibility of containing an adjective. An adjective also answers certain questions pertaining to nouns such as "Which one?" "What kind?" "How many?" "How much?" and "Whose?." Adjectives can also take on a variety of qualities, and the following examples show several of those different qualities.

Type	Examples
Comparative Adjectives **(Express a degree of comparison)**	The **taller** boy caught the ball. The **tallest** boy was not there.
Demonstrative Adjectives **(Express the concept of "pointing out")**	**This** truck is for sell. **These** cars are for sell.
Descriptive Adjectives **(Express some property of quality)**	The **blue** boat is docked. The **bathroom** sink is leaking.
Distributive Adjectives **(Express separation)**	**Either** movie will suffice. **Neither** person is in charge.
Interrogative Adjectives **(Express asking questions)**	**Which** teams were involved in the playoffs? **What** homes have you found?
Numerical Adjectives **(Express a number)**	**Two** men abducted the young girl earlier today. The student is in her **second** year of college.
Quantitative Adjectives **(Express a quantity or degree)**	**All** Americans should support that law. **Some** laws are better than others. We have **sufficient** food during this time of need.

Referring back to your sample sentence, how many adjectives can you identify?

The boy proudly gave Sally, a friend, the tiny bat and ball as her gift.

The sample sentence has only one adjective and it is "tiny." Label the adjective by simply writing "Adj" above it.

The boy proudly gave Sally, a friend, the <u>tiny</u> bat and ball as her gift.
Adj

You only have three words remaining that need identified. Take a look below.

Art   n   AV N Art n   Art Adj n   n   Pro n
The boy proudly gave Sally, a friend, the tiny bat and ball as her gift.

Practice

Directions: Identify the adjective(s) in the following sentences.

1. There are pretty flowers in your rose garden.

2. A few students went to see the Shakespearean play.

3. Which chapter did we have to read for English class?

Adverbs

Adverbs are like a sibling to adjectives as both function by modifying and describing. Arguably, adverbs are one of the most difficult parts of speech for students to identify as they modify or describe adjectives, verbs, and other adverbs. Like adjectives, they answer certain questions such as "How?" "When?" "Where?" and "To what extent?" And like some adjectives, some adverbs have the distinct "ly" ending. Take a look at the following sentence.

The <u>costly</u> loss was hard on the athlete.

In the sentence, the word "costly" is an adjective describing the noun "loss." Now, look at this next sentence.

She <u>easily</u> administered the test to the students.

In the second sentence, the word "easily" is an adverb describing the verb "administered." Look at how each word functions and what it modifies. For instance, you know that the word "easily" is not modifying the word "test" or even the word "students."

The word "not" is always an adverb. More importantly, the word "not" also helps reveal a distinct problem in formal writing: the contraction. Contractions should not be used, or should be used sparingly, in formal academic writing because they are slang.

INFORMAL: He doesn't go to the beach.

FORMAL: He does not go to the beach.

In the sentence, the word "not" is an adverb modifying the helping verb "does." You will also notice that the informal sentence is written as if you were talking to a friend. Some assignments in college will allow for informal writing and contractions, while others will not. It is important to know the difference between formal and informal in order to discipline yourself as a writer. Take a look at another example.

INFORMAL: We aren't happy.

FORMAL: We are not happy.

In the second example, the word "not" is an adverb modifying the linking verb "are." As you can see, the word "not" loves verbs, and you will usually find the word hanging around those verbs. So, now that you have an awareness of adverbs, take a look at the different types of adverbs as well as some examples of each.

Type	Examples
Adverbs of Degree (Express "to what extent?")	The students are **extremely** tired. He **greatly** exaggerated the story.
Adverbs of Manner (Express "how?")	He **heroically** saved the cat in the tree. She **quietly** studied in her dorm.
Adverbs of Place (Express "Where?")	The ship will dock **ahead**. She played **upstairs**.
Adverbs of Time (Express "When?")	Play **now**. She wrote to him **daily**.

As you can see, not all adverbs have the "ly" ending, but seeing certain words answering the questions "How?" "When?" "Where?" and "To what extent?" will help you identify adverbs. Referring back to the sample sentence in this chapter, do you see any adverbs in the sentence?

The boy proudly gave Sally, a friend, the tiny bat and ball as her gift.

The sample sentence has only one adverb and it is the word "proudly." Label the adverb by writing "Adv" above it.

Adv
The boy proudly gave Sally, a friend, the tiny bat and ball as her gift.

You only have two words in your sentence that are unidentified. Take a look.

Art n   Adv AV N Art n   Art Adj n   n   Pro n
The boy proudly gave Sally, a friend, the tiny bat and ball as her gift.

Practice

Directions: Identify the adverb(s) in the following sentences.

1. He cautiously went down the dark path.

2. Mary greatly admired her mother.

3. Jack's children always came first.

4. Move onward.

5. Fourth, we must quickly leave.

Conjunctions

As the name suggests, conjunctions are words that join other words, phrases, or clauses together in a sentence, but their functions vary. There are three types of conjunctions: coordinating, subordinate, and correlative.

Coordinating conjunctions include the words "for," "and," "nor," "but," "or," "yet," and "so."

Coordinating Conjunctions	
Function	**Example**
Joining Words	The boy **and** girl went home. (Joins the two words "boy" and "girl")
Joining Phrases	My cat loves having her head scratched **but** hates having her claws trimmed. (Joins the two verb phrases together)
Joining Clauses	Juan went to school, **but** Bonnie went to bed. (Joins the two independent clauses or two sentences together)

Next, subordinate conjunctions are words that begin dependent clauses (clauses that are not complete sentences) and join the dependent clause to an independent clause that the dependent clause needs in order to survive, or be part of a complete sentence, as you will learn later in this chapter. There are more subordinate conjunctions than there are coordinating conjunctions. The following list provides many examples of subordinate conjunctions, but it is still an incomplete list.

Subordinate Conjunctions
after, although, as, as if, because, before, even if, even though, if, in order to, once, provided that, rather than, since, so that, than, that, though, unless, until, when, whenever, where, whereas, wherever, whether, while, why

Finally, the correlative conjunctions are word pairs that work together to join elements in a sentence. The following list provides many examples of correlative conjunctions, but the list is incomplete.

Correlative Conjunctions
both/and, either/or, neither/nor, whether/or, not only/but also, such/that, so/as, no sooner/than

Referring back to your sample sentence in this chapter, do you see any conjunctions in the sentence?

The boy proudly gave Sally, a friend, the tiny bat and ball as her gift.

The sample sentence has only one conjunction and it is the word "and." Label a conjunction by simply writing "Conj" above it.

Conj

The boy proudly gave Sally, a friend, the tiny bat <u>and</u> ball as her gift.

Only the word "as" remains unidentified in the sample. Take a look.

Art   n   Adv   AV N Art n   Art Adj n Conj n   Pro n

The boy proudly gave Sally, a friend, the tiny bat and ball as her gift.

Practice

Directions: Identify the conjunction(s) in the following sentences.

1. Either Rick or Lacey will help you.

2. The mouse and rabbit ran away.

3. Maggie is a happy student, but Jason is a sad one.

4. John and Mary won't be attending the play because they are sick with the flu.

Prepositions

Prepositions are words that come before a noun or a pronoun to govern and express their relation to another part of the sentence. Prepositions also begin prepositional phrases, which will be covered in the next step of the process in this chapter. There are dozens of words that can serve as prepositions in a sentence. The following table provides a good, but incomplete, list of common prepositions that are used in writing.

Prepositions
aboard, about, above, across, after, against, along, amid, among, around, as, at, before, behind, below, beneath, beside, besides, between, beyond, but, by, concerning, considering, despite, down, during, except, excepting, excluding, following, for, from, in, inside, into, like, minus, near, of, off, on, onto, opposite, outside, over, past, plus, regarding, round, save, since, than, through, to, toward, towards, under, underneath, unlike, until, up, upon, versus, via, with, within, without

After looking at the list and all of the parts of speech up to now, you probably noticed something troubling: some words can serve as different parts of speech. For example, the words "but" and "for" can be either conjunctions or prepositions. As mentioned earlier, understanding the function of words will help you to identify parts of speech. You must understand the nature of the word and how it is operating. Take a look at the following two sentences that use the word "for" differently.

SAMPLE SENTENCE 1: Tom is tired, for he was working late last night.

SAMPLE SENTENCE 2: Tom gave Sally candy for Easter.

Can you tell which sentence uses the word "for" as a preposition and which sentence uses the word "for" as a conjunction and why? The trick in identifying whether a word is a preposition or a conjunction involves the part of speech of the word, or words, that come after it, so take a look at the first sample sentence. The word "for" begins the entire thought "for he was working late last night." Notice the helping verb "was" and an action verb "working" after the word "for." If a verb appears after the word in question, then that word in question can never be a preposition, because prepositions never have verbs after them that appear inside the entire thought being expressed. In this instance, the word "for" is being used as a conjunction joining two sentences, or independent clauses, together.

Now, revisit the second sample sentence and apply what you just learned. What is the entire thought being expressed by the word "for?" Here, the entire thought being expressed is "for Easter." As you can see, there is no verb after the word "for," only the noun "Easter." Therefore, this sentence is not combining two sentences. What you have here is a prepositional phrase, which will be discussed more in-depth in step two. After reviewing these two sample sentences, you are now ready to apply this knowledge to the sentence you have been working with since the beginning of this chapter:

The boy proudly gave Sally, a friend, the tiny bat and ball as her gift.

The sample sentence has only one preposition which is the word "as." This is a preposition because it has no verb after it, only the possessive pronoun "her" and the noun "gift." According to what you just learned, that is the strong indicator that makes this a preposition, along with it directing the noun "gift." Write "Prep" above the word "as" in order to label it.

Prep
The boy proudly gave Sally, a friend, the tiny bat and ball <u>as</u> her gift.

You did it! You identified every word in the sentence! Take a look.

Art n   Adv   AV N Art n   Art Adj n Conj   n Prep Pro n
The boy proudly gave Sally, a friend, the tiny bat and ball as her gift.

Practice

Directions: Identify the preposition(s) in the following sentences.

1. She is going home for Christmas.

2. He cut the grass before the storm.

3. The girl from Maine is smart.

4. After dinner, I am going to my friend's house.

Interjections

Unless they are contained in a quote, interjections, words that denote feeling or emotion, are rarely used in formal writing. However, some college instructors allow students to write informally for assignments such as personal essays. Take a look at some examples:

Interjections (Examples)
Oh! Ah! Look! Well done! Yes! No!

Advanced Concept: Verbals

After you have mastered the parts of speech, you can take your learning to the next step: verbals. There are three types of verbals that you should recognize: gerunds, participles, and infinitives. Each type of verbal comes with its own set of challenges, so paying attention to how verbals function is the key to successfully identifying and using them.

Gerunds are verbs that act as nouns and have a distinct "ing" ending. Therefore, whatever a noun can do, a gerund can do, and that is important in regards to functionality moving forward. Take a look at the following examples.

SAMPLE SENTENCE 1: Writing is tedious.

SAMPLE SENTENCE 2: I like playing.

SAMPLE SENTENCE 3: Use a pencil for testing.

Can you spot the gerunds, the verbs acting like nouns? In the first sentence, the word "writing" is the gerund; in the second sentence, the word "playing" is the gerund; and in the third sentence, the word "testing" is the gerund.

The next verbal is the participle. Participles are verbs that act as adjectives and have a multiple endings such as "ing," "ed," or other past tense endings. Therefore, whatever an adjective can do, a participle can do. Take a look at the following examples.

SAMPLE SENTENCE 1: I want jogging shoes.

SAMPLE SENTENCE 2: I was frightened.

SAMPLE SENTENCE 3: I have a broken ankle.

Can you spot the participles, the verbs acting like adjectives? In the first sentence, the word "jogging" is the participle. In the second sentence, the word "frightened" is the participle. In the third sentence, the word "broken" is the participle.

Although there is more to learn in regards to participles, such as the concepts of present and past participles, it is important to know this most basic concept of participles at this point.

The final verbal is the infinitive. Infinitives are unique because they combine the word "to" plus a verb after it, and it is important to know that both words make up the infinitive. Sometimes, students tend to confuse prepositions with infinitives, and the confusion stems from the word "to." If you happen to struggle between the prepositions and infinitives, just remember the key differences. The preposition "to" has either a noun or pronoun after it and never a verb. The infinitive "to" has a verb after it.

Infinitives can act as nouns, adjectives, or adverbs. Therefore, whatever a noun, adjective, or adverb can do, an infinitive can do. Take a look at the following example of an infinitive:

SAMPLE SENTENCE 1: I like to play.

Can you spot the infinitive, the verb acting like either a noun, adjective, or adverb? In the first sentence, the words "to play" combine to make the infinitive, which is acting as a noun. While this example may have been easy, infinitives functioning as either adjectives or adverbs can be rather difficult. Take a look at the second sample sentence:

SAMPLE SENTENCE 2: He had a morbid desire to prey on the weak.

In the second sentence, the words "to prey" combine to make the infinitive, which is acting as an adjective. How is it functioning as an adjective? Think back to what you have learned about adjectives earlier in the chapter. Adjectives answer certain questions such as "which one?" or "what kind?" In this case, the infinitive "to prey" is answering the question: "what kind of desire?" Finally, infinitives functioning as adjectives always come after the word they are modifying or describing, as is true in the sample sentence. Now, take a look at one more example of an infinitive:

SAMPLE SENTENCE 3: To prepare, we practiced.

The words "to prepare" combine to make the infinitive in the third sample sentence, and it is functioning as an adverb. How is it functioning as an adverb? Much like the previous sample sentence, you need to think back to what you have learned about adverbs earlier in the chapter. Like adjectives, adverbs also answer certain questions such as "How?" and "To what extent?" In this sample sentence, the infinitive "to prepare" is answering the question "to what extent?"

When identifying verbals in sentences, you can mark them however you wish. You can mark a gerund as "Ger" or as a noun. You can mark a participle as "Part" or as an adjective. You can mark the two-word infinitive as "Inf" or as the part of speech it is acting as, which is either a noun, adjective, or adverb.

If you're still struggling with verbals, you should practice identifying them more with the following practice sentences before continuing to work on the process. However, be cautious. Some sentences have tricks to see if you are paying attention to the functionality or not. For instance, a word that has an "ing" ending could mean it is either a gerund or a participle.

Practice

Directions: Identify the verbal(s) in the following sentences.

1. Playing is fun.

2. Basketball is the best sport to play.

3. The broken toy was fixed last week.

4. The cracked eggs were thrown away.

5. I won't be able to go to the boxing match.

6. I love drawing.

Step 2: Identifying the Sentence Parts

Now that you have identified the parts of speech, the next step in the process is the identification of sentence parts. You can already piece some of step two together because of what you have done in part one. To begin, the focus will be on six key sentence parts: subjects, verbs, compliments, prepositional phrases, appositives, and verbal phrases. You might notice a few familiar words here, since, in step one, you already identified the verbs and prepositions. Therefore, you can carry them over to step two on your practice sheet before you do anything else, so as you begin step two, your sentence should look like this:

                    V   Prep
The boy proudly gave Sally, a friend, the tiny bat and ball as her gift.

The order of operations for step two is as follows:

1. Verbs

2. Prepositional Phrases (if you have any)

3. Subjects

4. Compliments (if you have any)

5. Appositives (if you have any)

6. Verbal Phrases (if you have any)

Prepositional Phrases

A prepositional phrase is a group of words that begins with the preposition (which you have already identified) and ends with a noun or pronoun that it governs. You may recall the following sentence from a previous exercise, this time, with the prepositional phrase identified:

Tom gave Sally candy (for Easter).

Now, apply the same knowledge to the sample sentence on your practice sheet. The sample sentence should look something like this:

                    V   Prep Phrase
The boy proudly gave Sally, a friend, the tiny bat and ball (as her gift).

As you can see, the prepositional phrase begins with the word "as" and ends with the word "gift." The preposition "as" is not governing "her." The preposition "as" is directing the "gift." The word "her" is simply telling the reader who possesses, or will possess, the gift.

Subjects

Because you already found the verb in the sentence and marked it, you now have to figure out who or what is performing the action, the verb, in the sentence. However, it is not always easy identifying the subject of the sentence for some students. Usually, a sentence follows a simple formula (S + V + Complete Thought), but there are times where the formula is changed a bit with the verb coming before the subject (V + S + Complete Thought). Take a look at the following examples:

EXAMPLE 1: Dan played catch. (S + V + Complete Thought)

EXAMPLE 2: There are baseballs in the bag. (V + S + Complete Thought)

Sentences are words that are arranged a certain way to convey meaning. The arrangement might throw you off when identifying subjects, for example. If that happens, just remember to ask the important questions, "Who?" or "What?" In regards to the examples above, who played catch? Dan did. What are in the bag? Baseballs are.

Another issue that might arise in identifying subject is that a subject might not even be in the sentence at all. How is this possible? Take a look at the follow examples:

SAMPLE SENTENCE 1: Turn on the water.

SAMPLE SENTENCE 2: Write it down.

As you can see, both sentences seem to be missing a subject. Well, technically, they are not. The subject is implied. In the above two imperative sentences, sentences that convey a request or command, the implied subject is "you," which answers the question, "Who?" Who is to turn on the water? You are. Who is to write it down? You are. These sentences, written in the second person, have the understood subject "you."

Another thing to consider is that sentences can also have more than one subject, as in the following three sentences:

SAMPLE SENTENCE 1: Dianne and Lacey are going to the party.

SAMPLE SENTENCE 2: Tom went to the party, but Becky did not.

SAMPLE SENTENCE 3: We will eat when they arrive.

In the first sample sentence, "Dianne" and "Lacey" are both subjects. They are joined by the conjunction "and." Remember to ask the question, "Who is going to the party?" Dianne and Lacey are. The second sample sentence is a compound sentence (two sentences being properly joined together by a comma and coordinating conjunction). Because you are joining two sentences, both sentences follow the first of the variations of the formula you just read about (**S + V + Complete Thought** and **V + S + Complete Thought**). Therefore, you will also have two subjects. Who went to the party? Tom went to the party. Who did not? Becky did not. In the final sentence, you have a complex sentence, consisting of an independent clause ("We will eat") and a dependent clause, a clause that cannot stand on its own as an independent sentence ("when they arrive"). You will learn more about clauses later. For now, in order to identify the subjects, ask the following questions. Who will eat? We will eat. Who is going to arrive? They are. Therefore, you have two subjects in the sentence.

Here are a few final tidbits regarding subjects before getting into your sample sentence. First, subjects can never appear inside of prepositional phrases. Next, the word "there" can never be the subject of a sentence. Subjects can be nouns, pronouns, gerunds, or infinitives. Use these tidbits to help you moving forward.

Now check out your sample sentence. What word(s) serves as the subject of the sentence?

The boy proudly gave Sally, a friend, the tiny bat and ball as her gift.

If you asked the question "Who proudly gave Sally a tiny bat and ball?" then you probably came up with the answer "boy" as the subject of the sentence. The boy gave Sally a tiny bat and ball. Therefore, in regards to the sentence parts, you have identified the prepositional phrase, the verb, and the subject. You sample sentence should look like the following:

S   V   Prep Phrase
The boy proudly gave Sally, a friend, the tiny bat and ball (as her gift).

Compliments

When it comes to English and grammar, you have probably heard of direct and indirect objects. They are known as compliments because they help complete the thought or meaning of the subject and verb combination. In order to make the identification easier for you, it is important to go back to step one and see what type of verb you have, whether it was an action verb or a linking verb. After identifying the verb type, you can then proceed with either objects or predicate extensions (predicate nominative or predicate adjective).

Objects Appear After Action Verbs

To begin, a sentence does not always have an object after the action verb. There are two types of objects that exist after action verbs: direct objects and indirect objects. One of the best ways to remember objects is to think about Christmas or your birthday because in a sentence you will have the giver (the subject), the receiver (the indirect object), and that which has been given (the direct object). In regards to the order of a sentence, both objects appear after the verb, but the indirect object always appears before the direct object. Therefore, a sample formula for a sentence would look like this:

FORMULA: Subject + Verb + Indirect Object + Direct Object.

Before moving on, it is important to for you to know that objects can never appear inside of prepositional phrases, which will make your job easier in the identification process.

Now, take a look at the sample sentence below. Can you identify the components, specifically the direct and indirect object?

SAMPLE SENTENCE: Barry gave his friend the ball.

In the sentence, the indirect object is the word "friend" and the direct object is the word "ball." Another way to find the direct and indirect object is to ask the following questions after the verb:

DIRECT OBJECTS: S+V+ "What?"

INDIRECT OBJECTS: S+V+ "To Whom?"

Predicate Extensions Appear After Linking Verbs

Earlier in the chapter, you learned that a verb is sometimes referred to as a predicate. In fact, you will eventually need to identify important compliments that actually use the term "predicate" in their respected titles. Like objects, they are extensions of the subject and verb combination. Predicate extensions will always appear after linking verbs, and there are two types of predicate extensions that exist: predicate nominative and predicate adjective. Like objects, predicate extensions appear after the verb, but each one has a distinct function. Predicate nominatives rename the subject, while predicate adjectives describe the subject. Take a look at the sample sentences below to see how each predicate functions:

SAMPLE SENTENCE 1: She is a nice girl. (Predicate Nominative)

SAMPLE SENTENCE 2: She is nice. (Predicate Adjective)

In the first sample, the predicate nominative "girl" renames the subject "she" and the two words are connected by a linking verb. In the second sample sentence, the predicate adjective "nice" describes the subject "she" and the two words are connected by a linking verb.

Another way that can help you identify the predicate extension is to look back in step one and consider what parts of speech you identified. How will that help? Well, predicate nominatives can only be either nouns or pronouns while predicate adjectives can only be adjectives.

Now that you have read about compliments, apply what you have learned to your sample sentence. First, take a look at the verb. What type of verb was it: action verb or linking verb?

The boy proudly gave Sally, a friend, the tiny bat and ball as her gift.

Because the word "gave" is the only verb in the sentence and is an action verb, what follows, if you have any, are objects. You will not have any predicate extensions. Can you identify any objects in the sentence?

The sentence has an indirect object ("Sally") and two direct objects ("bat," "ball"). In this case, the conjunction "and" joined together two words ("bat" and "ball") that happen to be direct objects in the sentence.

```
     S          V    I.O.              D.O.     D.O.  Prep Phrase
```
The boy proudly gave Sally, a friend, the tiny bat and ball (as her gift).

Appositives

Simply put, appositives are words in a sentence that rename the words they follow. If you are using step one of the process, the parts of speech, as a tool to help you with this current step, it is important for you to know that appositives are nouns or pronouns that rename or clarify the nouns or pronouns they follow in a sentence. Take a look at the sample sentences:

SAMPLE SENTENCE: My daughter <u>Britt</u> is intelligent. (Appositive)

In the sample sentence, the word "Britt" is the appositive that follows and renames the subject "daughter." Appositives can also appear as phrases in sentences. Take a look at the following sample sentence:

SAMPLE SENTENCE: Daniel, <u>a boy in my class</u>, is intelligent. (Appositive Phrase)

In this particular example, the phrase "a boy in my class" follows and renames the subject "Daniel." Therefore, you have an appositive phrase in the sentence. You might even notice that the appositive phrase has the prepositional phrase "in my class" within it. You can have smaller phrases within larger ones, as this sample sentence demonstrates.

Take a look at your sample sentence for this chapter. Do you see an appositive or appositive phrase in it?

The boy proudly gave Sally, a friend, the tiny bat and ball as her gift.

The appositive phrase is "a friend." Your sentence should currently look something like this:

     S   V   I.O.   App Phrase   D.O.   D.O.   Prep Phrase
The boy proudly gave Sally, (a friend), the tiny bat and ball (as her gift).

In fact, you have successfully identified all of the sentence parts in this sample sentence. However, as discussed earlier in this chapter, you may come across verbals, and verbals can play a role in the sentence parts as well. Therefore, it is important to be on the lookout for any potential verbal phrases in the sentence before moving on the third and final step in the process.

Advanced Concept: Verbal Phrases

In step one, you were introduced to the advanced concept of verbals. In this step, you were informed that a subject can be either a gerund or infinitive, but when it comes to step two, your work with verbals might not be finished. When you have a verbal in a sentence, there is a chance you will have to identify a verbal phrase in step two. However, the verbal phrases are different than prepositional phrases. You will always have a prepositional phrase if you have a preposition in the sentence. You won't always have a verbal phrase if you have a verbal in the sentence. Just as there are three types of verbals, there are also three types of verbal phrases: the gerund phrase, the participle phrase, and the infinitive phrase.

The Gerund Phrase

When gerunds are accompanied by modifiers or objects, you will have a gerund phrase. Like prepositional phrases, gerund phrases end with an object called the object of the gerund. Unlike prepositional phrases, just because you have a gerund in the sentence does not mean you will have a gerund phrase. The following provides an example of a gerund phrase:

Ger   Obj
I like (eating pizza).

" Eating" what?

As you can see, the structure of the phrase is similar to that of a prepositional phrase where the phrase begins with the gerund and ends with its object.

The Participle Phrase

When participles are accompanied by modifiers or objects, you have a participle phrase. Like the prepositional phrase and gerund phrase, the participle phrase ends with an object called the object of the participle. Unlike prepositional phrases, just because you have a participle does not mean you will have a participle phrase. Take a look at the following sample example:

Part   Obj
(Riding his bike), he wrecked into a tree.

"Riding" what?

Even though participle phrases seem to be pretty self-explanatory and easy, they are not. They can be tricky. Take the following sample example, for instance:

Part   S   V
SAMPLE SENTENCE: The frightened dog ran away.

When working on the sentence parts, students may have the urge to jump and mark the sentence as having a participle phrase; therefore, the answer would look like the following sentence:

"Frightened" what?

INCORRECT: The (frightened dog) ran away.

However, there are many problems with this. Assuming you correctly identified "dog" as the "subject," you should recall from earlier in the chapter that subjects can only be nouns, pronouns, and gerunds (which function like nouns). Participles function as adjectives, and as you know, nouns (as well as pronouns and gerunds) and adjectives are not the same and cannot function together, especially in this example. Subjects can never be adjectives, and the following provides the correct markings for the sentence:

S   V
CORRECT: The frightened dog ran away. (No Participle Phrase)

Just because you had a participle in the sentence does not mean you are guaranteed to have a participle phrase.

The Infinitive Phrase

When infinitives are accompanied by modifiers or objects, you have an infinitive phrase. Infinitive phrases begin with the infinitive and end with an object called the object of the infinitive. Unlike prepositional phrases, just because you have an infinitive in a sentence does not mean you will have an infinitive phrase. Take a look at the following infinitive phrase:

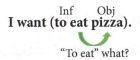

The structure of the infinitive phrase is just like all of the other phrases you have learned. However, you need to consider the concept of function before moving on to the next step. As you learned with the participle phrases, infinitive phrases can be tricky. Gerunds, and their phrases, can do whatever nouns can do. Participles, and their phrases, can do whatever adjectives can do. A participle cannot be the subject or object of the sentence, for example. Infinitives, and their phrases, can do whatever nouns, adjectives, and adverbs can do. Understanding the function will help you master advanced concepts such as verbal phrases.

Step 3: Clauses and Sentence Types

Clauses

A clause is a group of words that consist of a subject and a verb. There are two types of clauses, independent clauses and dependent clauses. As the name suggests, an independent clause consists of a subject, verb, and a complete thought. It can stand on its own. The following is the formula for an independent clause:

Subject + Verb + Complete Thought

A dependent clause consists of a subject, verb, and no complete thought. It cannot stand on its own. The following is the formula for a dependent clause:

Subject + Verb + No Complete Thought

In order determine how many clauses you have in a sentence, just look to see how many subject/verb combinations you have in the sentence. Finally, determine whether each clause has a complete thought or not so you can properly identify it as independent or dependent. Take a look at your sample sentence. How many subject/verb combinations do you have?

    S   V
The boy proudly gave Sally, a friend, the tiny bat and ball as her gift.

You only have one subject/verb combination with the word "boy" as the subject and the word "gave" as the verb, so you only have one clause. Now, let's proceed to sentence types.

Sentence Types

The four types of sentences are the simple sentence, the compound sentence, the complex sentence, and the compound-complex sentence. The type of sentence depends on the type of clause, or clauses, you have in a sentence. The following shows the formula for each sentence type:

SIMPLE SENTENCE = INDEPENDENT CLAUSE

Example: The clock was a gift from my parents.

COMPOUND SENTENCE = TWO INDEPENDENT CLAUSES

Example: The clock was a gift from my parents, but the chimes keep me up at night.

COMPLEX SENTENCE = INDEPENDENT CLAUSE + DEPENDENT CLAUSE

Example: The chimes keep me up at night because the clock is near my bedroom.

COMPOUND-COMPLEX SENTENCE = TWO INDEPENDENT CLAUSES + DEPENDENT CLAUSE

Example: The clock was a gift from my parents, but the chimes keep me up at night because the clock is near my bedroom.

Take a look at the following sample sentence one last time. What type of sentence do you have?

The boy proudly gave Sally, a friend, the tiny bat and ball as her gift.

The sentence is a simple sentence because it only has one independent clause. The other types of sentences will be addressed in the next chapter. Like building a house, you started with the most base components and built up to the very thing you will be writing in any essay: the sentence.

Step 4: Grammar Usage

Now that you have learned about what makes up a sentence, how it operates, and why, you must now move on to using this knowledge in your own writing. You are ready to add a fourth step to the three-step process, and this new step involves using grammar properly.

Using Proper Antecedent Agreement

When you use a pronoun, make sure the antecedent, or the word the pronoun stands for, is clear for your audience.

EXAMPLE: Troy told James that he needed to open his mind to constructive criticism and feedback.

Why is this sentence unclear? Do the subjective pronoun "he" and the possessive pronoun "his" refer to Troy or James? Is Troy referring to himself, that he needs to better accept criticism, or is he chastising James for not having an open mind? When using pronouns, make that your antecedent is clear, and, moreover, that one is present and near. Otherwise, your audience will not know what or whom you are referring to.

Directions: Identify the errors in the following sentences.

1. Anyone who volunteers in the hospital must present his badge.

2. The waves were very high, but it was calm by the end of the day.

3. Sue asked Jill if she could help her with her math.

In sentence one, do only men volunteer? A better way to write the sentence is "Hospital volunteers must present their badges." In sentence two, a plural pronoun, not "it," is required to agree with the plural antecedent "waves." The sentence can be correctly written as: "The waves were very high, but *they* were calm by the end of the day." In sentence three, who needs help with math? One way to rewrite the sentence is "Sue asked Jill if Jill could help her with her math." Make sure pronouns have clear antecedents, or your reader will be confused.

Using Comparative and Superlative Adjectives

Some students struggle with adjectives. When using comparative adjectives, you may have noticed that the suffix -er or -est is used to denote the comparative form and superlative form of an adjective, respectively. For example, the comparative form of "big" is "bigger." The superlative form of "big" is "biggest." You may also realize that the word "more" or "less" is used before some adjectives to denote the comparative form, while the word "most" or "least" denotes the superlative. When two elements are being compared, use the comparative form. The superlative form is used to compare three or more elements.

EXAMPLE 1: Sloths are slightly *slower* than turtles. Some experts say, however, that the sea anemone is the *slowest* animal in the world.

EXAMPLE 2: Hunting dogs are usually *less* affectionate than retrievers. Guard dogs typically are the *least* affectionate of all dogs.

Directions: Identify the errors in the following sentences.

1. Of the six European countries she had traveled to, Italy had the better food, she said.

2. Compared to my old car, the bus was most reliable for getting me to work on time.

3. Camille is the shyer of her three siblings.

Using "I" and "Me" Properly

Did you ever get confused as to when "I" and "me" in a sentence? "I" acts as the subject of the sentence and "me" acts as an object in the sentence.

Directions: Identify the errors in the following sentences.

1. Julia prepared most of the meal, but she graciously gave credit to Janise and I.

2. Josh and me went to the park yesterday.

Using Proper Subject and Verb Agreement

Students often make errors in grammar when using collective nouns. A collective noun is a distinct class of nouns that refers to a group of people, animals, or things. Examples of collective nouns are "team," "jury," "crowd," "committee," "herd," "class," "group," "gang," "flock," and "choir." Even though these nouns denote more than one member or object, they most often function as singular nouns in a sentence. For example, "The class delivered *its* assessment of the new teacher." The singular pronoun "its" agrees in number with the singular collective noun "class." The rule concerning collective nouns is this: if all of the objects or members of the collective noun are working together as one, as a single unit, then use a singular verb to agree with the collective noun, as well as a singular pronoun to take its place in the sentence.

EXAMPLE 1: The choir sings four acapella songs during the concert in its common room.

In this example, the singular verb "sings" and the singular pronoun "its" agree with the singular collective noun "choir." In the example sentence, "choir" acts as a singular collective noun because, as a unit, all of the members of the choir are singing, or performing the action. If members of the choir were performing or singing as individuals, then you would use a plural verb and pronoun.

EXAMPLE 2: The choir have been practicing their individual parts in the medley.

In the above example, all of the members are not acting as a unit; some or all may be acting independently. Therefore, you would use a plural verb ("have") and pronoun ("their"). Think of this sentence and its meaning this way: "They [individual choir members] have been practicing their individual parts in the medley." Perhaps a more agreeable, clearer way to write the sentence is "The members of the choir have been practicing their individual parts in the medley."

Directions: Identify the errors in the following sentences.

1. The jury waited for hours until their verdict was delivered.

2. We did not expect the split decision the committee has rendered.

3. The flock of seagulls have flown south for the winter.

Using Homophones Properly

Did you ever get confused as to which version of a word you should use, such as words like "their," "there," or "they're?" Well, you are encountering words that are known as homophones. They are words that sound the same but have different meanings and, usually, different spellings. Students often misuse homophones. The following chart provides some of the most common homophones as well as the proper spelling and meaning for each:

Homophone	Meaning
Affect **Effect**	The action of impacting something (usually a verb). The result of an action impacting something (usually a noun).
Aisle **I'll** **Isle**	A passage between rows of seats or shelves of goods in a building A contraction for the words "I will." A small island.
Cite **Sight** **Site**	To give credit as evidence in a source. The ability to see. A space of land where construction is usually planned.
Desert **Dessert**	An area of land that receives little water and has little vegetation. A sweet dish typically eaten after a meal.
Die **Dye**	To cease living. To color or change the color of something.
Dual **Duel**	Consisting of two parts. A fight between two individuals.
It's **Its**	A contraction for the words "it is." A possessive pronoun that expresses belonging.
Lessen **Lesson**	To make less or to diminish. An activity or learning period provided by an instructor.
Principal **Principle**	1: The person in charge of a school. 2: A sum of money. A rule, guideline, or fact.
Their **There** **They're**	A possessive pronoun that expresses belonging. Typically used as a noun or adverb regarding a place or position. A contraction for the words "they are."
Threw **Through**	The past tense form of the verb "throw." Movement from one side, or end, to another.

To	1: A preposition indicating motion. 2. Begins an infinitive.
Too	1: To express a higher degree of something. 2: Substitute for "also."
Two	The written equivalent for the number "2."
Vain	Excessive pride in one's appearance.
Vane	A device with flat components that is propelled by water or wind.
Vein	1: Blood vessels. 2: A layer of substance in the earth. 3: Of a similar style or mood.
Your	A pronoun expressing belonging or possession.
You're	A contraction for the words "you are."

Now that you have this chart as a reference, take a look at a few sample sentences that will demonstrate how homophones are misused and how they can be properly corrected.

Sample Sentence 1 (Incorrect): <u>Their</u> going to the store.

Sample Sentence 1 (Correct): <u>They're</u> going to the store.

Sample Sentence 2 (Incorrect): <u>You're</u> kite is stuck in the tree.

Sample Sentence 2 (Correct): <u>Your</u> kite is stuck in the tree.

In the first sample sentence, the word "their" is used incorrectly because "their" is a possessive form of the word "they." Therefore, the sentence would make no sense because you do not possess "going to the store." The writer means to say, "They are going to the store," so in order to fix the sentence, the homophone "they're" is needed. The second sample sentence used the contraction "you're" incorrectly. The sentence technically reads as "You are kite is stuck in the tree." Once again, this makes no sense. What the writer is intending to do in the second sentence is show possession of the kite. Therefore, in order to show possession of the kite, the word "your" is used to replace "you're."

Directions: Identify the errors in the following sentences. If the sentence is correct, then mark it as "Correct."

1. She would effect the outcome of the game.

2. I want to go to the game too.

3. The fighters engaged in an epic dual.

4. John through the ball to his teammate.

Class Exercise

Now that you have revisited basic grammar and sentence structure, go back to the opening "Unlearning" sentences. For steps one through three, apply what you've learned in this chapter regarding the three-step process and demonstrate that you understand the grammatical makeup of each sentence. Finally, in step four, correct the error(s) in each sentence.

SENTENCE 1

STEP 1: Identify the Parts of Speech

[Articles, Nouns, Pronouns, Verbs, Adjectives, Adverbs, Conjunctions, Prepositions, Verbals (Gerund, Participle, Infinitive)]

Me and my twin sister don't have the same hobbies and interests.

STEP 2: Identify the sentence parts

[Subjects, Verbs, Compliments (Direct Object, Indirect Object, Predicate Nominative, Predicate Adjective), Prepositional Phrases, Appositives or Appositive Phrases, and Verbal Phrases (Gerund Phrase, Participial Phrase, Infinitive Phrase)]

Me and my twin sister don't have the same hobbies and interests.

STEP 3: Identify clauses and sentence type

[Clauses (Independent, Dependent) and Sentence Type (Simple, Compound, Complex, Compound-Complex)]

Me and my twin sister don't have the same hobbies and interests.

STEP 4: Correct Usage

[Antecedent Agreement, Comparative and Superlative Adjectives, Use of "I" and "Me," Subject/Verb Agreement]

Me and my twin sister don't have the same hobbies and interests.

STEP 1: Identify the Parts of Speech

[Articles, Nouns, Pronouns, Verbs, Adjectives, Adverbs, Conjunctions, Prepositions, Verbals (Gerund, Participle, Infinitive)]

One of the boys left their cellphone on the bleacher.

STEP 2: Identify the sentence parts

[Subjects, Verbs, Compliments (Direct Object, Indirect Object, Predicate Nominative, Predicate Adjective), Prepositional Phrases, Appositives or Appositive Phrases, and Verbal Phrases (Gerund Phrase, Participial Phrase, Infinitive Phrase)]

One of the boys left their cellphone on the bleacher.

STEP 3: Identify clauses and sentence type

[Clauses (Independent, Dependent) and Sentence Type (Simple, Compound, Complex, Compound-Complex)]

One of the boys left their cellphone on the bleacher.

STEP 4: Correct Usage

[Antecedent Agreement, Comparative and Superlative Adjectives, Use of "I" and "Me," Subject/Verb Agreement]

One of the boys left their cellphone on the bleacher.

SENTENCE 3

STEP 1: Identify the Parts of Speech

[Articles, Nouns, Pronouns, Verbs, Adjectives, Adverbs, Conjunctions, Prepositions, Verbals (Gerund, Participle, Infinitive)]

The team will play their final game on Sunday.

STEP 2: Identify the sentence parts

[Subjects, Verbs, Compliments (Direct Object, Indirect Object, Predicate Nominative, Predicate Adjective), Prepositional Phrases, Appositives or Appositive Phrases, and Verbal Phrases (Gerund Phrase, Participial Phrase, Infinitive Phrase)]

The team will play their final game on Sunday.

STEP 3: Identify clauses and sentence type

[Clauses (Independent, Dependent) and Sentence Type (Simple, Compound, Complex, Compound-Complex)]

The team will play their final game on Sunday.

STEP 4: Correct Usage

[Antecedent Agreement, Comparative and Superlative Adjectives, Use of "I" and "Me," Subject/Verb Agreement]

The team will play their final game on Sunday.

SENTENCE 4

STEP 1: Identify the Parts of Speech

[Articles, Nouns, Pronouns, Verbs, Adjectives, Adverbs, Conjunctions, Prepositions, Verbals (Gerund, Participle, Infinitive)]

Otto worked relentless until the entire interior of the house was painted.

STEP 2: Identify the sentence parts

[Subjects, Verbs, Compliments (Direct Object, Indirect Object, Predicate Nominative, Predicate Adjective), Prepositional Phrases, Appositives or Appositive Phrases, and Verbal Phrases (Gerund Phrase, Participial Phrase, Infinitive Phrase)]

Otto worked relentless until the entire interior of the house was painted.

STEP 3: Identify clauses and sentence type

[Clauses (Independent, Dependent) and Sentence Type (Simple, Compound, Complex, Compound-Complex)]

Otto worked relentless until the entire interior of the house was painted.

STEP 4: Correct Usage

[Antecedent Agreement, Comparative and Superlative Adjectives, Use of "I" and "Me," Subject/Verb Agreement]

Otto worked relentless until the entire interior of the house was painted.

SENTENCE 5

STEP 1: Identify the Parts of Speech

[Articles, Nouns, Pronouns, Verbs, Adjectives, Adverbs, Conjunctions, Prepositions, Verbals (Gerund, Participle, Infinitive)]

Running toward the mountain, the cliffs appeared rugged and impassable.

STEP 2: Identify the sentence parts

[Subjects, Verbs, Compliments (Direct Object, Indirect Object, Predicate Nominative, Predicate Adjective), Prepositional Phrases, Appositives or Appositive Phrases, and Verbal Phrases (Gerund Phrase, Participial Phrase, Infinitive Phrase)]

Running toward the mountain, the cliffs appeared rugged and impassable.

STEP 3: Identify clauses and sentence type

[Clauses (Independent, Dependent) and Sentence Type (Simple, Compound, Complex, Compound-Complex)]

Running toward the mountain, the cliffs appeared rugged and impassable.

STEP 4: Correct Usage

[Antecedent Agreement, Comparative and Superlative Adjectives, Use of "I" and "Me," Subject/Verb Agreement]

Running toward the mountain, the cliffs appeared rugged and impassable.

Chapter [4]

Punctuation and Mechanics

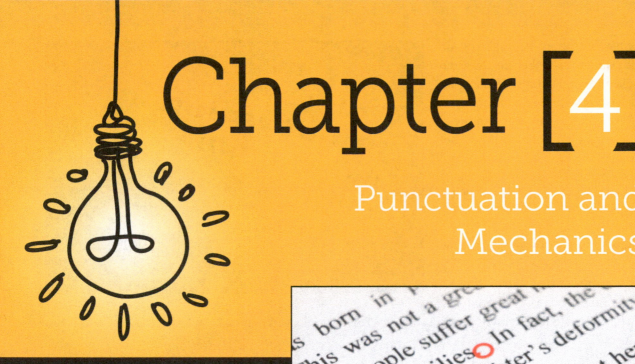

© Lamai Prasitsuwan/Shutterstock.com

Unlearning

Writing the way that you speak is the best way to approach academic writing. A run-on sentence is just a really long sentence and people get the message anyway. So what's the big deal? People of few words may speak in fragments and still get their point across. Sentence structure should not matter as long as content is heard and understood.

Relearning

You may know someone who is quite loquacious and continues to talk with pausing. After a while, do you stop listening? "Take a breath," you may think. As the listener, you may be the one who needs the breath, or series of breaths, because you need to time to comprehend and connect everything the speaker is saying. In fact, you may have stopped listening because you may be paying more attention to the person than what the person is saying.

The same is true when you read a text with run-on sentences. You notice the lack of pauses. You begin to pay more attention to lack of correct sentence structure than the sentence content and meaning. A period should be here, you think. A colon or dash should precede this listing of information. Your mind is diverted from what the person is saying to how the words are presented to you and that is a problem. You are no longer listening. Perhaps so much information is strung together that you would appreciate time to reflect upon what is written. Perhaps you do not even want to take the time to listen and make the connections. "This writer should have considered me more," you think. "Punctuations are signs for me to pause, stop, and consider. I should not have to take the time to backtrack and read unseparated independent clauses again in order to make sense of the narrative."

© TungCheung/Shutterstock.com

The same is true with fragments. Why should you have to take the time to figure out something that fails to convey a complete thought? Why should you need to backtrack to find a missing subject or verb? After a while, you may not want to continue. "This is too much work," you think.

While it is true that sometimes fragments can effectively be used to convey emphasis, your audience will accept this employment of a fragment if you have command of your sentence structure throughout the rest of your essay. Now that you understand the purpose of grammar from the previous chapter (parts of speech, sentence parts, clauses, and sentence types), and understand that this foundation is essential for building an effective essay, it is time to consider the importance of mechanics.

Owning a house will require you to become mechanically inclined in order to fix some of the things that might go bad over time. Sure, you can pay someone to fix these things for you. For writers who need help with mechanics, these repairers are called editors; but as a student, you don't have the luxury of professional editors fixing your work. You will need to become your own editor, and as you know, student writings often contain errors that must be corrected. When a paper has an abundance of mechanical errors, the reader becomes more focused on the errors rather than the content of the paper itself, so you are sabotaging your own work.

Much like what you did in the previous chapter, you will be building your knowledge of how to fix these errors from the bottom-up. Once you begin fixing these errors in sentences, you will move on to short paragraphs and eventually on to essays and other lengthy papers.

Punctuation

When writing, did you ever stumble on a moment when you did not know what punctuation to use? Did you ask, "Should I use a colon or a semicolon? Do I use a comma here or not?" Hopefully, you will have a clearer understanding of the punctuations after reviewing this section, which is devoted to those sometimes troublesome punctuations. The following chart provides a nice reference for you.

Punctuation Name	Punctuation Mark	Purpose
Period	.	Used at the end of a sentence to stop it.
Comma	,	Used to denote a contextual pause or a listing.
Question Mark	?	Used at the end of a sentence that asks a question.
Exclamation Mark	!	Used at the end of a sentence to express strong emotion.
Colon	:	Used within a sentence before a listing, quote, or explanation.
Semicolon	;	Used to connect independent clauses (simple sentences) as well as connect two or more parts in a sentence that are closely related in sequence or meaning.
Apostrophe	'	Used in a word to indicate possession or the omission of letters.
Quotation Marks	" "	Used in a sentence to denote another person's words.
Round Brackets	( )	Used in a sentence to provide additional information.
Square Brackets	[ ]	Used within a quote to provide additional information that did not appear in the original quote.
Ellipses	…	Used within a quote to denote the absence of an unspecified number of words, sentences, or paragraphs. Three dots signify deleted text within a sentence, while four dots reveal omitted words between sentences.
Hyphen	-	Used to join two words together.
Slash	/	Used to signify words that are alternatives.

Now that you have a listing of each punctuation mark and an explanation for its proper use in writing, take a look at the following examples to see how the punctuation marks may appear in writing:

Punctuation Name	Punctuation Mark	Example
Period	.	Tabitha and Jamie went to the store.
Comma	,	Robbie, Mark, and Trey sold tickets. (Listing) Maggie, my daughter, is very shy. (Contextual Pause/Appositive)
Question Mark	?	Why are you here today?
Exclamation Mark	!	I'm free!
Colon	:	Tom has three daughters: Jill, Melanie, and Jackie. (Listing) She kept screaming: "I'm not guilty!" (Quote) The general had one thought: to end the war. (Explanation)
Semicolon	;	She is tired; however, I am not.
Apostrophe	'	Welcome to Sarah's club. (Possession) I can't believe this! (Absence of letters/Contraction)
Quotation Marks	" "	Jon Smith said, "Where's the food?"
Round Brackets	( )	Max (also called "Tiny") is a tough fighter.
Square Brackets	[ ]	Larry said, "Samantha [Smith] is very friendly."
Ellipses	…	Maddie explained, "I'm tired….the trip just wore me out."
Hyphen	-	In order to get some good food, we'll have to go off-campus.
Slash	/	I'm going with Mike and/or John to the party.

Commas Rules

When do you need a comma and when do you not? The following rules and the practices should help to refresh your memory and provide you with the knowledge you need in order to strengthen your writing mechanics.

Rule #1

Use commas when you list three or more items in a sentence.

The rule is self-explanatory. Take a look at the following example:

INCORRECT: Jane, Mary, Lynn and Sara went to the store.

CORRECT: Jane, Mary, Lynn, and Sara went to the store.

With a listing of four people (Jane, Mary, Lynn, and Sara), insert a comma between the names of all four individuals, so you will include three commas. At times, the listings will be a little more complex. You might list prepositional phrases or gerund phrases, but what is important is that you remember the simple comma rule at this time: separating listings of three or more items with commas. If you feel as though you need some practice, work on the following section:

Practice Sentences

Directions: Correct the following sentences by adding the commas where necessary. If the sentence is correct, write "Correct."

1. Ben gave a gift to Jen Ali and Brooke.

2. Ian John and Mike went to the show.

3. Lenny provided Jake, Tom, and Jane with the classwork they missed.

4. The manager threw Chad Becky and Sarah out of the store.

5. I am friends with Justin, Paul, and Ron.

Now, check over your work. Sentences one, two, and four contain comma errors. In the first sentence, place a comma after the words "Jen" and "Ali." In the second sentence, a comma is needed after the words "Ian" and "John." Finally, in the fourth sentence, a comma should appear after the words "Chad" and "Becky." Sentences three and five are correct.

Rule #2

Use a comma and a coordinating conjunction to join sentences together.

Back in grade school, you may have heard the lyrics, "Conjunction Junction, what's your function?" There is a proper way to join sentences together that involves using both a comma and coordinating conjunction, but before you do so, you should determine if you definitely have two independent clauses, or two complete sentences to join. Therefore, you will want to check and see how many independent clauses you have in the sentence. Remember, an independent clause consists of a subject, verb, and complete thought. Take a look at the following example of this rule being applied incorrectly and correctly:

SENTENCE: <u>Tommy went to the store</u> but <u>Joyce went home</u>.
COMPLETE THOUGHT   COMPLETE THOUGHT

INCORRECT: Tommy went to the store but Joyce went home.

CORRECT: Tommy went to the store, but Joyce went home.

Because the sample sentence contains two independent clauses, both the comma and the conjunction are needed to properly join these clauses. Simply writing the coordinating conjunction "but" between them will not properly join them together; you will have committed the error of writing a run-on sentence (two or more sentences that are incorrectly joined together). Additionally, you cannot just connect the two independent clauses with a comma because you will have then committed the error of writing a comma splice (two or more sentences that are incorrectly joined together with only a comma and not a coordinating conjunction).

Why join sentences together with a comma and conjunction? The answer is very simple: it drastically improves the readability. Imagine separating the sentence into two. Using the same sample sentence, read the following:

SENTENCE: Tommy went to the store. Joyce went home.

Imagine reading an entire paper written like this. It would have no flow. It would be choppy. There would be a lack of connection, logic, and sequence between thoughts. Thanks to modern word processing software, improving your paper's flow and readability by adding a comma and coordinating conjunction (for, and, nor, but, or, yet, so) to join sentences takes only seconds.

Furthermore, sentences combined with a comma and coordinating conjunction function better than that of two sentences combined with a semicolon. Semicolons are reserved for certain circumstances. For instance, semicolons that combine two sentences are effective when those two sentences are very closely related. Take a look at the following example:

SAMPLE SENTENCE

Some homeowners prefer hardwood floors; others prefer carpeting.

As you can see from the example sentence, the two sentences that are combined with a semicolon are closely and logically related. The problem with the use of semicolons is the effect it has on flow or readability. In order to help maximize your readability, the example sentence should be rewritten:

REVISED SAMPLE SENTENCE

Some homeowners prefer hardwood floors while others prefer carpeting.

With this rewritten sentence, the semicolon was replaced with the subordinate conjunction "while." The subordinate conjunction reveals the relationship between the two independent clauses. In addition, notice the improvement in sentence flow.

Practice Sentences

Directions: Combine the following sentences by adding a comma and/or coordinating conjunction where necessary. If the sentence is correct, write "Correct."

1. Bre wasn't hungry so I picked up a fork and ate her pasta.

2. I may consider your idea or I may not.

3. Lacey wants to attend college, but she hasn't met all of the requirements.

4. The delivery van ran out of gas. The pizza was hot.

5. I will be late for the show. I am working until seven tonight.

Now, check your answers. The only sentence that is correct is sentence three. In sentence one, add a comma before the conjunction "so" because you cannot join two independent clauses with only a conjunction. You need the comma. In sentence two, add a comma before the conjunction "or." In sentence four, eliminate the period and join the sentences together by adding a comma and conjunction. In order to show the relationship between what initially may appear to be two unrelated independent clauses, an appropriate revision to sentence is this: "The delivery van ran out of gas, but the pizza was hot." Notice how the use of the comma and conjunction better connects and conveys meaning between the clauses—in this case, revealing that the result (hot pizza) was unexpected due to the delayed delivery. In sentence five, eliminate the period once again and add a comma and conjunction. An appropriate revision to the final sentence is, "I will be late for the show, for I am working until seven tonight." Again, the use of the comma and conjunction better reveals the relationship between the clauses. You more readily understand that the subject will be late for the show because she is working late. A period between the independent clauses does not connect the thoughts or show relatedness between the separate clauses as well.

Rule #3

Use a comma to separate two or more adjectives describing the same word.

As you have already learned in Chapter 3, adjectives are used to modify or describe nouns in a sentence. Sometimes, writers like to use multiple adjectives to describe the same noun. When you use two or more adjectives to equally describe the same word, you separate them using a comma. Take a look at the following example of this rule being applied incorrectly and correctly:

INCORRECT: The weatherman is predicting a long cold winter.

CORRECT: The weatherman is predicting a long, cold winter.

In the sample sentence, both adjectives, "long" and "cold," equally describe the noun "winter," and so they must be separated with a comma.

However, you might not like the idea of more commas in a paper. After all, each writer has his or her own style. Luckily, the mechanics of grammar provide options that you can use. You are not forced to fix the two adjectives using only this method. There is another way. Rather than add a comma between the two adjectives, simply write the conjunction "and" between them. Look at this alternate way to write the sentence:

SENTENCE: The weatherman is predicting a long and cold winter.

Which way do you prefer: using the comma or the word "and?" It is really your call because both ways are mechanically correct. Now, test your knowledge by completing the following practice sentences.

Practice Sentences

Directions: Correct the following sentences by adding the commas where necessary. If the sentence is correct, write "Correct."

1. He descended into the damp, cold dungeon.

2. My tall handsome date had no personality.

3. Jack is a young, smart kid.

4. The soft cool breeze was refreshing.

5. The house has a bright red room.

Sentences one and three are correct. Sentence two needs a comma between the adjectives "tall" and "handsome." Sentence four requires a comma between the adjectives "soft" and "cool." Finally, in sentence five, add a comma between the adjectives "bright" and "red."

Rule #4

Use a comma for an introductory word, phrase, or dependent clause that appears before the independent clause.

Writers sometimes like to begin a sentence using an introductory word, phrase, or dependent clause. If or when you decide to do that, just make sure to put a comma after the introductory word, phrase, or dependent clause. Take a look at the following example of this rule being applied incorrectly and correctly:

INCORRECT: Due to inclement weather the game was postponed.

CORRECT: Due to inclement weather, the game was postponed.

In the sample sentence, the independent clause is "the game was postponed." The introductory component in the sentence, sometimes referred to as the condition, is "due to inclement weather." Therefore, you must insert the comma at the end of the introductory component and before the independent clause.

However, you might not want a lead-in word, phrase, or dependent clause. You might prefer to begin your sentence with the independent clause. Choosing to do so is your choice as a writer and is also allowed according to the rules of mechanics. Using the exact same sentence you just used, read the following:

SENTENCE: The game was postponed due to inclement weather.

Choosing to move the introductory item to the end of the sentence does not require you to use a comma. Here is the rule: when a condition appears at the beginning of a sentence, you put a comma after it; when a condition appears at the end of a sentence, you do not need a comma.

Practice Sentences

Directions: Correct the following sentences by adding the commas where necessary. If the sentence is correct, write "Correct."

1. When the time is up I will sound the alarm.

2. If the weather is nice, we should go to the park

3. She will stop over for a visit when she returns from her trip.

4. During the summer I like to play baseball.

5. After the storm we can go outside and play.

Now, check to see how you did. Sentences two and three are correct. Sentence two correctly has a comma after the opening condition. Since, in sentence three, the condition "when she returns from her trip" comes after the independent clause, no comma is needed. However, sentence one needs a comma after the word "up" because "When the time is up" is a condition that appears before the main, independent clause. In sentence four, place a comma after the word "summer" because "During the summer" is an opening condition appearing before the independent clause. Finally, add a comma after the word "storm" in sentence five.

Rule #5

Use commas before and after words, phrases, or clauses that are not essential to the meaning of the sentence or the reader's ability to identify a particular person, place, or thing.

Each sentence that you write should have meaning. The meaning of each sentence will be a part of a greater whole, whether that work is an essay, research paper, or a book. However, writers usually add details to the sentence that are not essential to the overall meaning. Nonessential details can be written as words, phrases, or even clauses, and the best way to gauge whether they are essential or not is to remove them from the sentence to see if the meaning changes. If the meaning changes, then the details are essential. If the meaning does not change, then the details are nonessential. Therefore, as the rule states, you use commas before and after words, phrases, or clauses that are not essential to the meaning of the sentence or the reader's ability to identify a particular person, place, or thing. The following is sentence contains nonessential information set off by two commas.

SAMPLE SENTENCE 1: Always strive to treat people better than they treat you, as my father used to say, because you will have peace of mind about your words and actions.

Notice that the words "as my father used to say" function as information nonessential to the overall meaning of the sentence.

Similarly, use commas around an appositive that is nonessential to identifying the noun that precedes it. For example, because of his notoriety and achievements, Tom Brady is a well-known and recognized quarterback. Therefore, the appositive in the following sentence is not needed.

SAMPLE SENTENCE 2: Tom Brady, the football player, won his fifth MVP Super Bowl award during his first year with the Tampa Bay Buccaneers.

Notice that the appositive "the football player" is nonessential information in this sentence for two reasons. Not only is Tom Brady well known and identifiable, but also the context of the sentence, specifically the words "Super Bowl," already identifies Brady as a football player. When it comes to appositives and the use of commas, context matters.

Before moving on to more mechanical rules, test your knowledge of commas with a comprehensive practice, a short paragraph that contains an error from each of the five comma rules.

Practice Paragraph

Directions: Identify the comma errors in the paragraph.

Before leaving their hometown Logan Beth and Paul wanted to say "goodbye" in their own way. Logan the oldest child went to the beach for it was his favorite place. Beth's favorite place was a deep dark cave in the nearby woods. Finally Paul went to the local coffee shop where he spent many hours talking with his friends. Everyone has his or her own way of saying "goodbye" and Logan Beth and Paul were no exception.

Correcting Fragments, Run-ons, and Comma Splices

Fragments, run-ons, and comma splices are three of the most common errors in student writing. Thankfully, they all can be readily fixed.

Fragments

A fragment is an incomplete sentence, and so something is missing from it, such as a subject, a verb, or both. If you think you might have a fragment in your writing, try to identify the subject and verb in the sentence, and then read it to see if it is a complete thought. Take a look at the following sample fragment errors:

FRAGMENT 1: Missed class yesterday. (Missing subject)
V

FRAGMENT 2: The students with their notebooks. (Missing verb)
S

FRAGMENT 3: Including teachers and students. (Missing subject and verb)

When you read each fragment, you should be able to tell that something is missing, and that is why each example is not a sentence. In the first fragment, the subject is missing. Who was missing class yesterday? In the second fragment, the verb is missing. What did the students do with their notebooks? Finally, the third fragment is missing both the subject and the verb. You are only provided with a phrase, and as you know by now, a sentence requires a subject, verb, and a complete thought. Fragments can easily be converted to complete sentences with simple subject and/or verb additions.

FIXED FRAGMENT 1: Jerry missed class yesterday.
S   V

FIXED FRAGMENT 2: The students fanned themselves with their notebooks.
S   V

FIXED FRAGMENT 3: Everyone went, including teachers and students.
S   V

Now, you can test your knowledge of fragments by completing the following practice sentences.

Practice Sentences

Directions: State what is missing from each fragment (subject or verb), then correct each fragment by adding the missing subject or verb. Answers will vary.

1. Randy laughing at his brother.

2. Plays the organ.

3. Mary to earn her degree.

4. The police chasing the thief.

5. Missed the shuttle bus.

In sentence one, the verb is missing or, at least, worded poorly. Therefore, change "laughing" to "laughed": "Randy laughed at his brother." Next, sentence two is missing a subject. With sentence three, a simple re-wording will suffice: "Mary will earn her degree." The problem in sentence four is another missing or poorly worded verb. Changing "chasing" to "chase" converts a fragment, an incomplete thought, into a complete thought, a sentence. The final sentence is missing a subject, so you would have to add a subject to let the reader know who missed the shuttle bus.

Run-ons

A run-on consists of two or more sentences that are incorrectly joined together. Unlike fragments, run-ons are complete sentences, so they do have subjects, verbs, and complete thoughts. The problem is that they do not have proper punctuation to separate the independent clauses, and thus multiple sentences are incorrectly joined. Take a look at the following sample run-on and read it aloud:

RUN-ON: The jogger was getting tired he had completed the second mile he was unable to finish the race.

After reading it aloud, you probably paused at places where a pause, or punctuation, was needed. However, there are no pauses. The independent clauses just keep going, running into each other, which is why they are labeled run-ons. Refer back to the sample sentence. Determine how many sentences are in the run-on by identifying the number of subject/verb combinations that have complete thoughts. After you do so, you will find something like this:

              S   V   S   V   S   V

RUN-ON: The jogger was tired he had completed the second mile he was unable to finish the race.

As you can see, the sample run-on has three subject/verb combinations, and each combination has a complete thought. Therefore, each combination is an independent clause and a sentence. The good news is that there are a variety of ways to fix this sentence. There are four primary ways to fix a run-on sentence. You may add a period to stop a sentence. You may add a relative pronoun or subordinate conjunction in front of the independent clause to turn it into a dependent clause. You may separate two of the clauses with a semicolon. Finally, you may even combine sentences using a comma and conjunction. The following is just one way to fix the sample run-on sentence:

FIXED RUN-ON: The jogger was tired. He had completed the second mile, but he was unable to finish the race.

The sample run-on was fixed using two methods. Between sentence one and two, a period was added. Between sentence two and three, a comma and conjunction were added. However, these four solutions are somewhat basic. If you wanted, you could add and subtract words as well as reword elements to make it all work for you. Work on the following sentences for more practice.

Practice Sentences

Directions: Fix each run-on. Answers may vary.

1. The class ended we left and went home.

2. An operation is necessary that is what the doctor said.

3. Heather reported the robbery to the police and the officer said he would investigate.

4. The sun came out so we went to the park.

5. I'm not going to the party tonight I am tired.

Possible Solutions

For sentence one, probably the best way to fix the run-on is to add a comma and the conjunction "so" after the word "ended." Sentence two has multiple options for a fix. One way to fix sentence two is to reword it and say, "The doctor said the operation is necessary." Another way to fix sentence two is to simply add a period after the word "necessary," and then capitalize the word "that." Even though the sentences will be short and choppy, they would be mechanically correct. Sentence three simply needs a comma added before the conjunction "and" to make a compound sentence using a comma and conjunction. For sentence four, add a comma before the conjunction "so" to properly combine the two sentences. Finally, sentence five can be fixed a few ways. One of the more popular ways to fix the sentence is to reword and reorganize it to say, "I am tired, so I'm not going to the party tonight." Remember, the explanations provided are not the only ways to correct each of the sentences. Other ways do exist. Consider which way is most appropriate for your assignment, context, or narrative voice and style.

Comma Splices

A comma splice is a type of run-on sentence in which two sentences are joined together only by the use of a comma, which is mechanically incorrect. Take a look at the following sample comma splices:

COMMA SPLICE 1: The jogger was tired, he had completed the second mile.

COMMA SPLICE 2: He had completed the second mile, he was unable to finish the race.

In order to determine if you have a comma splice or a complete sentence, you will once again seek out the subject/verb combinations. Then, you will need to determine if each subject/verb combination expresses a complete thought. After you examine both sample sentences, each of them should have the following markings:

S   V   S   V

COMMA SPLICE 1: The jogger was tired, he had completed the second mile.

S   V   S V

COMMA SPLICE 2: He had completed the second mile, he was unable to finish the race.

The bottom line is this: you cannot join two sentences together with a comma. Fix comma splices the same way you fix run-ons, using any one of the four techniques. Once again, you could add a period to stop a sentence, add a relative pronoun or subordinate conjunction in front of the independent clause to turn it into a dependent clause, separate two of the clauses with a semicolon, or combine sentences using a comma and conjunction. The corrected sample sentences would look something like the following:

FIXED COMMA SPLICE 1: The jogger was tired after he completed the second mile.

FIXED COMMA SPLICE 2: He had completed the second mile but was unable to finish the race.

For the first corrected comma splice, the word "after" was added to turn the second half of the sentence into a dependent clause. The most notable fix for the second corrected comma splice is the deletion of the comma and addition of the conjunction "but."

Practice Sentences

Directions: Fix each comma splice. Answers may vary.

1. Dogs offer wonderful companionship, they also offer great stress relief.

2. She went to basketball practice, she did not do her homework.

3. Mark loves traveling, he also likes good food.

4. I'm exhausted, I want to go to bed.

5. In a few days, I want to go to the grocery store, I also want to go to the mall.

The best way to correct each of the comma splice errors is to add a fitting contextual conjunction after each comma. For sentence one, the conjunction "and" works well after the comma. You can add the conjunction "but" after the comma in sentence two, the conjunction "and" in sentence three, the conjunction "and" in sentence four, and the conjunction "and" after the second comma in sentence five. However, you are not limited to simply adding a conjunction after the comma. If you are aware of another mechanically acceptable way of fixing the comma splice, you are allowed to explore that option as well.

Now, test your knowledge of fragments, run-ons, and comma splices with a comprehensive practice, a short paragraph that contains each of the errors.

Practice Paragraph

Directions: Identify the fragment, run-on, and comma splice errors in the paragraph.

The big game. Jake was the star basketball player he was 6'8' and he was the lead scorer. The other team had no chance against Jake and the Warriors, they had no player who could beat Jake on the court. The Spartans had John Smith but he was only 6'2 he was only a sophomore. As predicted, the Warriors won the game 78-42 it wasn't even close.

Using Parallel Structure

When you use parallel structure in your writing, you are basically making parts of the sentence structurally or rhythmically identical by using the same grammatical form, and this greatly enhances the readability. What does that mean exactly? Take a look at the following sentence:

SAMPLE SENTENCE 1

The man was small, had a round figure, and he was rude. (Lacking Parallel Structure)

Even though the sentence is mechanically sound, it lacks parallelism and reads poorly. Notice the listing of "small," "had a round figure," and "he was rude." Each has its own unique grammatical form. The word "small" is an adjective. Next, the phrase "had a round figure" is a verb phrase. Finally, the words "he was rude" is a clause because it has a subject and a verb. When you write, all three elements in a listing should have the same (parallel) form, so either write all three as adjectives, verb phrases, or clauses. For example, the following sentence was rewritten so that all three elements in the listing are adjectives. Take a look at the corrected sample sentence:

SAMPLE SENTENCE 1

The man was small, round, and rude. (Contains Parallel Structure)

Notice how well the sentence reads now! As many English experts say, "it has balance." However, you have the freedom to choose your own words when considering parallel structure. If necessary, find better, more appropriate words. For instance, maybe you don't like the word "round." Maybe you have a better word in mind. You are allowed to replace the word with a better, more appropriate one. Take a look:

SAMPLE SENTENCE 1

The man was small, portly, and rude. (Contains Parallel Structure)

As you can see, the word "portly" might read as more descriptive to some readers. Descriptive and professional word choices are most often encouraged.

Because parallelism can be a difficult concept to grasp, take a look at one more example:

SAMPLE SENTENCE 2

Jane is not only the president of our club but also city council president. (Lacking Parallel Structure)

Unlike the first sample sentence, this sentence only has two elements in the listing. You want parallel structure, so choose either nouns or prepositional phrases to make the construction parallel. Take a look at the corrected sentence:

SAMPLE SENTENCE 2

Jane is president not only of our club but also of the city council. (Contains Parallel Structure)

As you can see, the listing now reads "of our club" and "of the city council," and both elements are now prepositional phrases rather than two different grammatical forms.

Practice Sentences

Directions: Correct the following sentences by giving each listing proper parallel structure. If the sentence is correct, write "Correct." Answers may vary.

1. The baseball fans jumped and were applauding the homerun.

2. It is best to study for a test over time rather than cramming the night before.

3. Driving to a destination is sometimes cheaper than it is to fly.

4. I like playing soccer and to fly internationally.

You could have corrected the first practice sentence one of two ways. First, you could have written "The baseball fans jumped and applauded the homerun" or "The baseball fans were jumping and applauding the homerun." Rewrite the second sentence either as "It is best to study for a test over time rather to cram the night before," or "It is best studying for a test over time rather than cramming the night before." Sentence three can be written to incorporate parallel structure the following ways: "To drive to a destination is sometimes cheaper than it is to fly," or "Driving to a destination is sometimes cheaper than flying." Finally, sentence four could be revised as, "I like playing soccer and flying internationally," or "I like to play soccer and to fly internationally."

Hopefully, this chapter refreshed your memory regarding punctuation and the mechanical concepts of writing, and perhaps you learned something new. When you begin to write your papers, you can always refer back to this chapter and check your work to see if your sentences are mechanically sound. In time, the goal is that you can become self-reliant with your writing and acquire the confidence and ability to be your own personal editor.

Chapter [5]
Structure Building

© GaudiLab/Shutterstock.com

Unlearning

Every essay must be comprised of five paragraphs and follow the introduction, body, conclusion format. Every paragraph must have a concluding, summary sentence. You must write a formal outline before you begin your essay.

Relearning

Now that you have poured the foundation for your house (Chapters 3 and 4), you are ready to start building the frame and the structure. Setting up a game plan for your writing only makes sense. This does not mean that, unless you have had specific instructions from your instructor, you must adhere to a rigid outline and a certain number of paragraphs. Nor should you feel compelled to end each paragraph with a summary sentence. Allow yourself the freedom to come up with your own plan and structure that is dictated by the requirements of your assignment, your content, and your individual style. Accordingly, it usually is not a good idea to plan and write your paper the day before it is due. In sports, teams prepare to succeed in upcoming games by studying films and subsequently arriving at a game plan of their own. In preparing to write an essay, you need a similar game plan, one that prepares you for the best way to build your structure and communicate your message.

This chapter focuses on the writing process and structural elements you should consider as you make a game plan when preparing to write a college essay.

College Writing: The Writing Process

To be an effective writer, you need to understand that writing is a process, often a back and forth process, that requires much preparation, time, and thought. Applying the writing process provides a great, general plan for any writer. First, examine the writing assignment. What is your purpose? What is your point of view? What is your thesis, claim, or main idea? Who is your audience? How do you gain credibility? How will you support your thesis? These are all important questions to ask and answer before you write a word. In fact, you must understand your purpose for writing, and often arrive at you thesis statement, or main idea, before you begin to write. If you do not know your purpose or have not composed a clear thesis, then what are you writing about? Always remember your purpose as you set up your essay's structure. Your purpose is reflected in your thesis, which, in essence, is a contract you have with your audience. Your thesis sets up expectations about what your purpose is in your essay. Your audience will hold you to these expectations.

As you consider more preliminary plans, you may think about how you are going to support your claims or fulfill the promises you made in your thesis statement. You may want to do some outside reading if you are working on a research paper. If you are responding to an essay, you will want to read the essay carefully and plan to use textual evidence to support your point of view. You may think about how you will organize your thoughts, whether by listing ideas sequentially or by writing a loose or formal outline, whatever works best for you.

In the next step of the writing process, you do the obvious: write! If you had composed an outline, do not be restricted or limited by what you had written in the planning process. Allow yourself to push past preliminary boundaries you had set for yourself as you discover more through research or see more as you concentrate on the essay in front of you. The third step of the writing process involves examining the content of your paper. How successful have you been in supporting your thesis? Arguably, this is the most difficult step for many writers.

The final step of the writing process is polishing your essay. You want to ensure that the mechanics of the paper are sound. You may examine your word choice or diction, phrasing, and sentence fluidity. The following graphic provides a visual representation of the writing process:

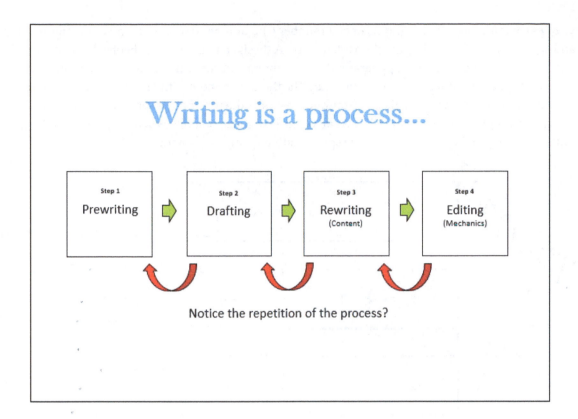

Take notice of the red arrows moving backward. One of the best aspects about the writing process is that you can stop, go back, and rework any part of the process whenever it is necessary.

College Writing: The Essentials

Before you begin surveying some of the larger aspects of writing, review the basics first and really understand the parameters. For instance, a sentence is a group of words that has a subject performing an action and is expressed in a complete thought. A sentence is a clause, or a group of clauses, that always has to have at least one independent clause. Furthermore, a sentence can be expressed as either an assertion, a question, an exclamation, a command, or as a wish. A sentence begins with a capital letter and ends with the appropriate punctuation mark.

Next, consider the paragraph. A paragraph is a group of sentences, traditionally five or more sentences, that specifically focuses on one main idea. A paragraph is identified with a new line as well as an indentation or numbering. A paragraph also contains a topic sentence that states the main idea of the paragraph and can technically appear anywhere in a paragraph, although it traditionally appears toward the beginning. The main idea of a paragraph is the author's direct or implied message stating what the paragraph is about. When the main idea is implied, you will have an implied topic sentence. Therefore, the topic sentence is not directly stated to the reader. Paragraphs grow longer and become more developed due to the supporting sentences, the several sentences that back the main idea in the topic sentence. Additionally, if it fits your purpose, you might choose to include a concluding sentence that indicates the closure of the paragraph to readers, and, even better, one that transitions or leads smoothly to the first sentence of your next paragraph.

Finally, an essay is a group of paragraphs of any number (the number depending on your assignment, purpose, and style) that is governed by the thesis statement. A thesis statement is the theory that you are advancing in your essay and traditionally appears as the last sentence in the introductory paragraph, although it may effectively appear in other places in your essay. The thesis statement is the main idea of the entire essay. In regards to its structure, an essay has, at minimum, an introductory paragraph, a body paragraph, and a concluding paragraph. So generically, what do all of the essentials look like when they are pieced together? The following table provides a sample visual representation of an essay's structure.

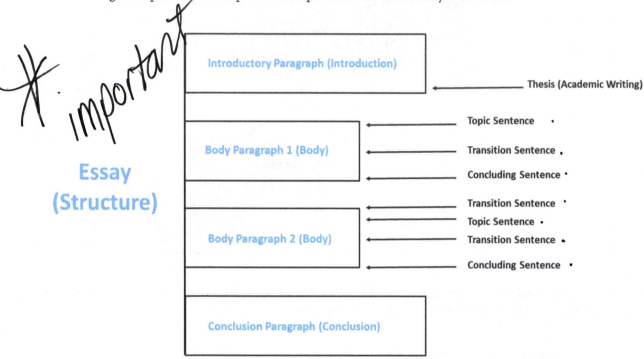

As you advance through writing, you will discover that you can have multiple paragraphs for the introduction, body, and conclusion. One particular assignment that permits a multiparagraph introduction, body, and conclusion is the research paper. A master's thesis, a doctorate dissertation, and a book will all have a multi-paragraph introduction, body, and conclusion.

Working with Structure

The structure of a composition can be achieved in a variety of ways. Sometimes an outline works for one paper, but it doesn't work for another. Some students are gifted storytellers, while others are not. Each student is different and, in fact, each assignment is different. Therefore, the best way to determine structure is by assessing your situation.

For instance, if you are assigned a reflective or narrative essay to write, a plot outline might help you achieve some semblance of structure for your essay. After all, most stories follow a plot outline, even though some do it in their own unique way. The plot outline consists of the background, which is sometimes referred to as the exposition. The exposition provides the necessary background information vital for audience understanding. The next component introduces a conflict or problem in the story that the characters have to overcome. The rising action consists of the events that occur before the climax. The climax is the part of the story that changes everything, and it is the decisive event that turns the story around. The falling action consists of the events that occur after the climax, and finally the resolution is the conclusion of a story, the time in which the conflict is resolved. However, the question still remains: how can this help your writing?

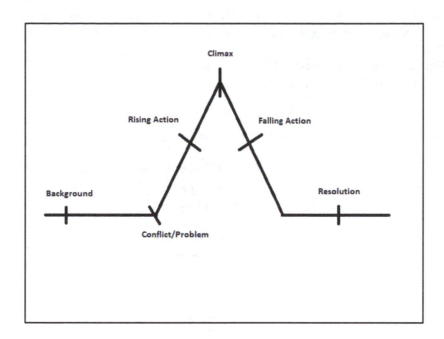

One potential way a plot outline can help structure your writing is to envision each component as its own paragraph. Since there are six components to a plot outline, you might plan to write six paragraphs. You do not have to restrict yourself this way; for example, the rising action section of your story may require multiple paragraphs. Furthermore, you may find that, due to multiple events occurring before and after the climax, you need multiple paragraphs for both the rising and falling actions of your story. On the other hand, you might choose to include the conflict or problem in an introductory paragraph with the background information. Then, you would have a five-paragraph essay. The plot outline can help serve as a solid base from which to launch your narrative or reflective writings. You may find a better way to structure more academic based writings.

For more academic-style papers, a thesis statement alone might be enough to help structure your paper. In order to understand how that works, you will need to understand the structure of a thesis statement first. Good thesis statements are usually written in a single sentence that contains the follow three components in it: the topic, the assertion, and the divisions of proof. The topic should be a specific title given to the subject matter being discussed. Meanwhile, the assertion is the opinion or claim you are trying to convey and prove to the readers. Finally, the divisions of proof provide your reasons for making the assertion, which is where you can generate the structure of your paper—from the divisions. In other words, the divisions of proof can serve as the blueprints for your paper, an unofficial table of contents. Consider the following thesis statement, for example:

SAMPLE THESIS: Native American names, mascots, and logos should be banned from sports teams because they perpetuate the Native American stereotype as aggressive and antagonistic, they depict cartoonish rather than authentic images of lifestyle and tradition, and they mock more than honor indigenous people.

This thesis beautifully sets up the essay's structure. The divisions of proof (perpetuation of the stereotype, cartoonish instead of authentic images, and the mocking instead of honoring) define and demarcate the distinct body paragraphs that will follow the essay's introduction. Each division of proof may comprise one or several paragraphs. Each, however, will follow the sequence that has been set up in the thesis statement.

However, situation matters. When assigned a shorter writing, each division of proof will likely become a single paragraph. Take a look at the sample thesis statement:

Topic   Opinion   Division of Proof

SAMPLE THESIS: John Smith University is an affordable choice for higher education.

The sample thesis statement only presents a single division of proof: "...an affordable choice for higher education." Your first option is to simply go with a three-paragraph essay with the single division of proof serving as your body paragraph, so the structure of the essay would appear like the following:

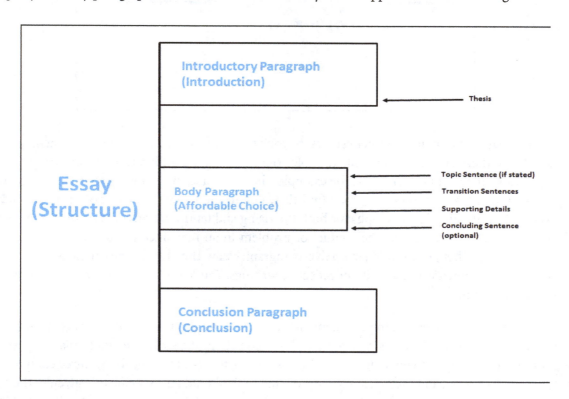

Again, another option is to explore the thesis a bit further and expand upon the supporting details, which will require more paragraphs or divisions of proof. Why is John Smith University an affordable choice? You might come up with several reasons and rewrite your thesis to include each of them, or you might choose to keep the thesis the way that it is and include several paragraphs (one or more for each reason). Perhaps the first body paragraph will compare John Smith University's cost to all of the other local colleges and universities while a second body paragraph might compare John Smith University's costs to similar universities across the country. Therefore, you would have a four-paragraph essay with the introduction, two body paragraphs, and the concluding paragraph. Visually, the essay would look like the following:

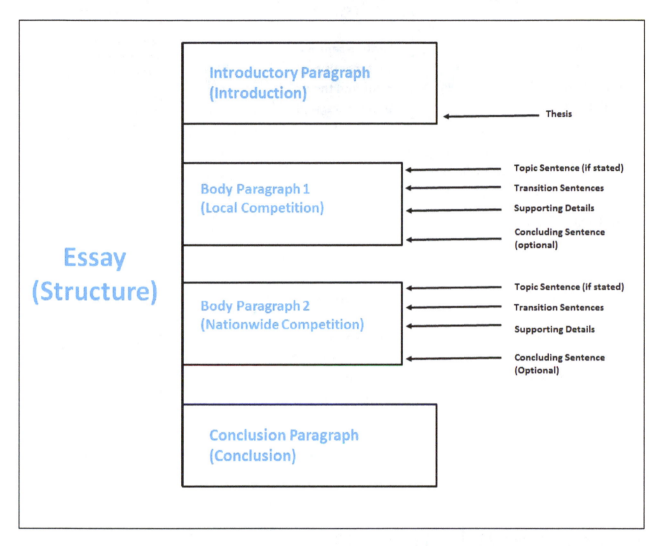

Finally, when you are assigned lengthier writings such as research papers, each division of proof will likely become multiple paragraphs.

Working with Main Ideas

Once you have composed a draft of your essay, make sure your main ideas are present and clear. The main ideas of a paragraph manifest in the form of a topic sentence. Additionally, you will also need to make sure your essay's main idea is pervasive throughout the essay, or, in other words, that you have fulfilled the expectations promised in the thesis sentence, whether that thesis statement is direct and clear or implied. Remember, you set up expectations with your thesis or implied purpose. Do not let down your audience. Fulfill the terms of your direct or implied contract, or your audience will be disappointed.

Main Idea of Each Paragraph

STEP 1		STEP 2		STEP 3
Read the paragraph you wrote and identify its topic and point.		Write a sentence that identifies the topic and the point of the paragraph.		Stated: The sentence in the paragraph resembles the one you wrote. Unstated: The sentence you wrote is the implied main idea of the paragraph.

Main Idea of an Essay

STEP 1		STEP 2		STEP 3
Read the essay you wrote and identify its topic and point.		Write a sentence that identifies the topic and the point of the essay.		Stated: The sentence in the essay resembles the one you wrote. Unstated: The sentence you wrote is the implied main idea of the essay.

Working with Transitions

In film and television, scenes often transition with the use of a fade or wipe. Sports even have their own versions of transitions between innings, quarters, and periods. Compositions are no different. In writing, transitions come in different forms such as words, phrases, or even sentences, but they all serve the same purpose: to smoothly move from one idea to the next. Transitions help readers understand the relationship and sequence of ideas in your writing. Because words have different meanings, they have different functions, and the same is true of transitional words. The following chart provides examples of transitional words according to their function and meaning.

TRANSITIONAL WORDS	
Transitions of Causation	because; consequently; therefore; thus
Transitions of Chronology	about; after; as; during; final; first; immediately; last; later; meanwhile; next; now; often; previously; second; simultaneously; soon; until; when; while
Transitions of Clarification	indeed; specifically
Transitions of Conclusion	accordingly; lastly
Transitions of Contrast	although; conversely; despite; however; nevertheless; otherwise; still; yet
Transitions of Location	above; across; against; behind; below; beyond; here; nearby; opposite; over; overhead; there
Transitions of Similarity	additionally; again; also; another; besides; furthermore; likewise; moreover; next; plus; similarly

Like words, phrases also have different meanings. The following chart provides examples of transitional phrases according to their function and meaning.

TRANSITIONAL PHRASES	
Transitions of Causation	as a consequence; as a result; at last; resulting in; so then
Transitions of Chronology	as soon as; at the same time; in the future; to begin
Transitions of Clarification	for example; for instance; in fact; in other words; in reality; that it; to clarify; to demonstrate; to explain; to explain further; to illustrate; simply stated
Transitions of Conclusion	in closing; in short; in summary; in the end; to conclude
Transitions of Contrast	counter to; even though; in spite of this; on the contrary; on the one hand; on the other hand
Transitions of Location	next to; to the left; to the right; to the front; to the back
Transitions of Similarity	along with; as well as; equally important; for example; for instance; in addition

Including transitional sentences in your writing will help readers with the logic and flow of your composition. You may even pick up or repeat a word, several words, or a theme from the previous paragraph to make the transition to the next paragraph a smooth and logical conversion. Immerse your readers in a continuous flow of sentence rhythm, sequence, and logic to keep them focused on your point of view and purpose. A lack of transition often serves as a stop sign or detour taking your reader down another road. That road is the realization that something structurally, sequentially, or logically is not right, and the focus, for your audience, is no longer on what you are trying to show or prove, but on the disruption along the way. Do not divert your readers' attention by unintentionally leading them down that other road. If you repeatedly divert their attention, they may not care to get back on track.

Chapter [6]

Embracing the "I" (First-Person Point of View)

© Bonuseventus/Shutterstock.com

Unlearning

In high school, you may have been told *never* to use the first person point of view, or the pronoun "I," in academic writing. Forget that instruction immediately. In fact, when your writing project essentially demands it, embrace your "I" voice.

Relearning

Now play this out: if your instructor asks you to write an academic essay describing a series of events or a singular moment that made you change, or led you to reconsider, your original point of view, would you use the third person, singular pronoun "he" or "she" to describe what happened to you? Why would you distance yourself that way from not only your audience, but also your personal experience and your position? Surely you would not use the third-person pronoun "they," since the last time you checked, you were only one. Similarly, why would you push your experience onto your audience by using the second person pronoun, "you," as if your audience experienced what you experienced vicariously? When relating a first-hand experience, the use of the pronoun "I" coveys both authenticity and immediacy.

For example, Wes saw a bear when he was in the woods. What point of view would be most appropriate for him to describe what he saw?

(1) I jumped off a tree branch and, after I hit the ground, I looked up into the concave face of a grizzly.

(2) You jumped off a tree branch and, after you hit the ground, you looked up into the concave face of a grizzly.

(3) He jumped off a tree branch and, after he hit the ground, he looked up into the concave face of a grizzly.

By using first person, the reader obviously knows that Wes expresses what he, himself, has experienced. This situation happened to Wes, and the use of "I" adds legitimacy and nearness to the encounter. He thrusts us not only into the action of the event but also, potentially, into *his* observations, *his* mindset, for his is the genuine experience. He was there. Furthermore, had he used the second person ("you") or third person ("he") point of view, Wes would have distanced himself instead of establishing himself as the expert as to what had happened.

Perhaps you did not fully understand what your instructors meant when they told you not to use first-person narration for certain assignments such as summaries, lab reports, or research papers. When you summarize, you are restating an author's main ideas in your own words. Since your own assumptions and opinions should not appear in the summary, there is no reason to use the pronoun "I." Summaries require an impression of objectivity in that you are following an author's order and emphasis. Generally, creators of lab reports and scientific writing also strive to remain objective in showing data and outcomes. Should the first-person (subjective) point of view appear, the data or results may appear tainted or biased. Research writing is a type of formal academic writing in which the weight of your personal anecdotes may be questioned relative to the credible, recognized sources you are citing to advance the purpose of your research. One person's experience, or even your individual experience, may be considered unreliable or, at the very least, not a representative sample. Research writing itself denotes that you, as a writer, are searching beyond your own realm of knowledge and understanding to become more informed about a topic. The surrender of the "I," then, suggests a search for, and an accumulation of, information beyond your own.

First, ask yourself this general question when you are considering what point of view to use: For this assignment, is the focus more on me or on the work or topic? When you write a critique, you are asked to analyze a passage for the significance, accuracy, clarity, logic, and use of information. The focus, then, is on the work itself, which suggests that you will avoid a first-person perspective. However, a critique also requires your response to the presentation. At this point in the paper, when you show agreement with the author's conclusion, or disagreement with validity of the author's examples, or invoke counterclaims based on your experience, the first-person point of view may be appropriate.

Second, evaluate the other opportunities and reasons to embrace your "I." Let's look at some of them.

1. Personal Anecdotes

Personal observation, reflection, self-expression and self-definition essays call for a first-person, active perspective: first person because the writer herself lived through the complications she describes; active because this type of writing is different from business writing. Look at the difference the "I" perspective makes in second student's response (Response B) to the diagnostic, the friend's question to the student as to why English composition courses should be forced upon them. Earlier in the essay, when the writer says she was forced to read *The Fountainhead*, she says, "In high school, I didn't like the idea the binding was so tight so that I had to pull the pages apart to read the last words of the left page lines and the front words of the right page lines." Notice not only the active sentence structure (person performing the action), but also how relatable the writer's voice is. Compare that to one of her later sentences about why we should be forced to read ("Form letters cannot be read to one by secretaries over the phone"). In this latter sentence, the student abandons the "I" and uses passive voice, and the response comes off as rather stodgy and formal, like something a member of a committee might say. Perhaps she thought, based on what she learned in high school, that this is how she was supposed to write a college paper. Now compare both sentences, from the same response, to assess clarity and impact. How does the sentence about form letters unable to be read answer the prompt about required composition classes? How does it make sense in general?

Ask yourself this question: Do I naturally talk this way to a friend? This leads us to the second reason to embrace the "I."

2. When It Is Appropriate to Use Your Speaking Voice Rather Than a More Formal, Academic Voice

Look again at the responses to the diagnostic prompt in Chapter 2. How do you respond to a friend—more like the writer of Response A ("The masses need to heed this: today we must all work together to perform all kinds of tasks that must be done to avoid disaster, chaos, and tragedy") or like the writer of Response C ("I feel you, man")? Your voice and tone (attitude toward your subject) should enhance, not distract your audience from your purpose.

3. When the Work Requires Your Opinion

When rendering your opinion, it seems logical to embrace the "I." How many times do we say "I think" or "I believe" when espousing our opinion or blowing off steam? Often, our opinions are biased, based solely on personal experiences, preference, or sheer appeals to emotion (pathos). In many cases of formal writing, however, restraint is necessary. When writing an argument essay, your audience may discount your opinion or experience as one of many, and claim that it, in and of itself, is not weighted or representative enough to persuade. Arguments are constructed with not only appeals to emotions, but also with ethical appeals (ethos) and logical appeals (logos). We rely on credible sources, logic, and multiple points of view to show both sides of an issue and to derive fair, balanced conclusions. Never do you want to disrupt a rational approach to your argumentation with what your audience may hear as an intrusive tone or unsupported assertion. What might your audience say if all of your examples for your argument are derived from your own experience? How do the use and consideration of multiple sources and perspectives make an argument fairer?

Remember, you can also convey personal experience without using first-person narration. For example, in an observation essay, you may simply describe "what happened," or what you witnessed, without using the first person pronouns I, me, my, mine, we, our, ours, and us: "All of a sudden, the bus stopped, the doors opened, and the passengers, hands over their faces, jumped off and ran down the busy street."

On the other hand, many students mistakenly equate formal writing with third-person point of view. Formal writing does not preclude the use of first-person narration. In fact, most insight, definition, identity, reflection, observation, and self-discovery essays are formal in tone and are written using the first-person perspective. There are other occasions to use first-person narrative than those mentioned above.

When considering point of view, always think about your purpose and the level of objectivity required for your task. Hopefully, you will have many opportunities to embrace the "I" in your writing and discover that when you find your voice and purpose, something important comes to the surface, something urgent is at stake for you, and your writing will matter both to you and your audience.

Look closely at one type of personal narrative, the reflection essay, and how you may come to a better understanding of yourself through the process of writing.

THE REFLECTION ESSAY

Unlearning

Now that you know you can embrace your "I," here are other convictions you may have that you can now unlearn for the reflection narrative.

1. You must first write an outline.

2. You need an explicit thesis at the start of the essay.

3. Keep to the five-paragraph essay.

4. You must end each paragraph with a repeating, summary sentence.

5. Repetition in an essay is always unnecessary.

6. Simply telling is interesting.

Relearning

First things first: you are released from outline prison. You are welcome.

There are certainly valid reasons why you were asked to write an outline. Perhaps the first outline you composed was in grade school. You did not know how to start your essay because you never wrote one before. Your teacher assured you that an outline would help you to organize your thoughts and think about the order and prioritization of the information you would later present. You found that writing the outline was harder than writing the actual essay. In fact, when writing your outline, you had to think, in a condensed sort of way, about each part of the essay. You had to think about a topic, an introduction and thesis, a few body paragraphs, some filler or details, and a conclusion that would restate what you already said. When you actually had to write your essay, *you didn't have to think much at all*. You just followed the points of your outline and, voilà, you were done.

Surely, having an organizational plan is a good thing. At this stage of the game, however, not having to think much at all as you write because you are rigidly following your outline is not such a good thing. In fact, you may be missing out on many opportunities to reflect and discover more about yourself through the process of writing. One word may lead to another, or to an image, or to an observation which did not come to you as you were preparing your outline. An outline may constrain you from further, deeper, self-reflection.

On the other hand, some students are able to compose an outline and go beyond its boundaries and delve deeper into their reflections and explore even more as they write. Do not limit yourself to what you jotted down in your outline. Allow your words and images to grow as you write. Allow yourself to think, to connect, to discover.

Perhaps you should also unlearn that an explicit thesis statement must always appear at the beginning of your essay, usually as the last sentence of your first paragraph. For many academic essays, this general rule serves a purpose: the thesis orients your reader and sets up expectations about the content and organization of your piece. A deductively arranged essay presents the thesis first and then supports that thesis with subsequent examples, anecdotes, or facts. In many personal essays, however, a beginning thesis may not be such a good idea. The thesis may give too much away to your audience concerning where you are headed in your essay, as well as the outcome; or it may limit you in discovering more yourself through the process of writing. For example, if you tell your audience what lesson you learned at the beginning of your essay, what comes next may be anticlimactic for them, since you have already told them the resolution or lesson learned. You want to develop conflict or narrative tension to keep your audience interested; preliminary blatant foreshadowing or outright telling in your thesis may very well dilute that suspense. You may want to reserve your thesis until the end. In an inductively arranged essay, you tell, or better yet, *show* the story (more on this later) and subsequently your main idea, or thesis, can be identified, or often better yet, understood, at the end. Notice we say "understood" and not "explicitly stated." You may come right out and state your thesis if that is the best way, you believe, to conclude your essay. However, in personal essays, the thesis is often implicit. If you have done a good enough job in showing—in building characterization, conflict, tension, and resolution—your audience will know the theme and purpose of your essay without your needing to hit them over the head with an obvious reminder. Often, your readers, themselves, would rather come to understand and *feel* your main idea without more intervention from you. If you can earn that understanding and feeling from your audience, you have succeeded.

You may also unlearn some past remedial structural suggestions now that you are in college. The five-paragraph essay model (an introductory paragraph, three body paragraphs, and a concluding paragraph) has also been referred to as the hamburger model. Between the buns, or your intro and conclusion, are three more layers, the "meat" and condiments, or flavor, of your essay. Grade-school composition instructors often encourage the five paragraph essay to show the value of solid introductions, textual support, sequence, transitions, and conclusions. The five-paragraph essay also encourages concise writing, the type of academic writing favored with standardized testing. However, after eating hamburgers all the time, you want to try something else, right? Why, with all of the prompts you will be asked to respond to, should you be constrained to five paragraphs? Your structure should depend on your purpose, your audience, and, most of all, *you*, and how you tell your story and find it best to arrange your narrative sequence.

Similarly, you do not need to conclude each paragraph with a summary sentence. Especially with personal writing, summation sentences in paragraphs seem unnecessary and overly formal. If you are engaging your audience, your audience will remember what you just said. We may even be frustrated by what we feel are sentences that actually take us away from your story's "meat." So it may be time to take off your training wheels and allow yourself to find the structural balance that works best for you in fulfilling your narrative purpose.

Although you need not repeat yourself in concluding sentences, not all repetition in composition writing is bad. In fact, foreshadowed and repeated images, allusions, words, and themes may work wonders to help you achieve your purpose. Let's look at how author Gary Soto, in his essay, "The Pie," relates a defining moment in his life, in large through the use of repetition.

The Pie

Gary Soto

I knew enough about hell to stop me from stealing. I was holy in almost every bone. Some days I recognized the shadows of angels flopping on the backyard grass, and other days I heard faraway messages in the plumbing that howled underneath the house when I crawled there looking for something to do.

But boredom made me sin. Once, at the German Market, I stood before a rack of pies, my sweet tooth gleaming and the juice of guilt wetting my underarms. I gazed at the nine kinds of pie, pecan and apple being my favorites, although cherry looked good, and my dear, fat-faced chocolate was always a good bet. I nearly wept trying to decide which to steal and, forgetting the flowery dust priests give off, the shadow of angels and the proximity of God howling in the plumbing underneath the house, sneaked a pie behind my coffee lid Frisbee and walked to the door, grinning to the bald grocer whose forehead shone with a window of light.

"No one saw," I muttered to myself, the pie like a discus in my hand, and hurried across the street, where I sat on someone's lawn. The sun wavered between the branches of a yellowish sycamore. A squirrel nailed itself high on the trunk, where it forked into two large bark-scabbed limbs. Just as I was going to work my cleanest finger into the pie, a neighbor came out to the porch for his mail. He looked at me, and I got up and headed for home. I raced on skinny legs to my block, but slowed to a quick walk when I couldn't wait any longer. I held the pie to my nose and breathed in its sweetness. I licked some of the crust and closed my eyes as I took a small bite.

In my front yard, I leaned against a car fender and panicked about stealing the apple pie. I knew an apple got Eve in deep trouble with snakes because Sister Marie had shown us a film about Adam and Eve being cast into the desert, and what scared me more than falling from grace was being thirsty for the rest of my life. But even that didn't stop me from clawing a chunk from the pie tin and pushing it into the cavern of

From *A Summer Life* by Gary Soto. Copyright © 1990 by Gary Soto. Reprinted by permission.

my mouth. The slop was sweet and gold-colored in the afternoon sun. I laid more pieces on my tongue, wet finger-dripping pieces, until I was finished and felt like crying because it was about the best thing I had ever tasted. I realized right there and then, in my sixth year, in my tiny body of two hundred bones and three or four sins, that the best things in life came stolen. I wiped my sticky fingers on the grass and rolled my tongue over the corners of my mouth. A burp perfumed the air.

I felt bad not sharing with Cross-Eyed Johnny, a neighbor kid. He stood over my shoulder and asked, "Can I have some?" Crust fell from my mouth, and my teeth were bathed with the jam-like filling. Tears blurred my eyes as I remembered the grocer's forehead. I remembered the other pies on the rack, the warm air of the fan above the door and the car that honked as I crossed the street without looking.

"Get away," I had answered Cross-Eyed Johnny. He watched my fingers greedily push big chunks of pie down my throat. He swallowed and said in a whisper, "Your hands are dirty," then returned home to climb his roof and sit watching me eat the pie by myself. After a while, he jumped off and hobbled away because the fall had hurt him.

I sat on the curb. The pie tin glared at me and rolled away when the wind picked up. My face was sticky with guilt. A car honked, and the driver knew. Mrs. Hancock stood on her lawn, hands on hip, and she knew. My mom, peeling a mountain of potatoes at the Redi-Spud factory, knew. I got to my feet, stomach taut, mouth tired of chewing, and flung my Frisbee across the street, its shadow like the shadow of an angel fleeing bad deeds. I retrieved it, jogging slowly. I flung it again until I was bored and thirsty.

I returned home to drink water and help my sister glue bottle caps onto cardboard, a project for summer school. But the bottle caps bored me, and the water soon filled me up more than the pie. With the kitchen stifling with heat and lunatic flies, I decided to crawl underneath our house and lie in the cool shadows listening to the howling sound of plumbing. Was it God? Was it Father, speaking from death, or Uncle with his last shiny dime? I listened, ear pressed to a cold pipe, and heard a howl like the sea. I lay until I was cold and then crawled back to the light, rising from one knee, then another, to dust off my pants and squint in the harsh light. I looked and saw the glare of a pie tin on a hot day. I knew sin was what you took and didn't give back.

Discussion Questions

1. What words and images are repeated in this essay? How do these repeated words and images specifically serve Soto's purpose?

2. How many Biblical allusions can you find? How do these references, either singly or repeated, contribute to the essay's tone?

3. Look at the time progression in the essay, from before the theft, to the stealing and consumption of the pie, and to the aftermath, when the pie is gone. How does Soto build conflict throughout this sequence? What is the conflict in "The Pie"?

4. Some may label this piece as a self-definition essay. How old do you believe Soto was when he stole the pie? What clues in the essay define his age? After reading this essay, written by an adult looking back at a childhood incident, how might you see Soto now? What in the essay helps you to define him?

5. What other sensory words and images contribute to tone? Look specifically at the sights, tastes, smells, sounds, and textures.

6. How does Soto use secondary characters, such as the grocer, the neighbor, and Cross-Eyed Johnny? Are they more than random characters?

7. Soto shows more than he tells. Retell this story to a friend. For example, you may say, "When Soto was a child, he was bored and stole a pie. Then he felt guilty about it." How does telling lose the narrative's impact? Why is showing a good strategy to engage an audience? Go back to a few sections of the narrative and rewrite the sentences by telling instead of showing. For example, after Soto devours the pie, he says, "A burp perfumed the air." What does this burp symbolize? Would telling what Soto felt here be as impactful as the burp?

Let's look at how another writer defines herself. In the "[me]" chapter of *Bad Feminist*, Roxane Gay delivers a candid self-analysis in her essay, "Typical First Year Professor." As you read her essay, ask yourself the following questions. How does Gay develop her character and narrative voice? How does she keep you engaged? What does she show instead of tell? What is the effect of her ending image?

Typical First Year Professor

Roxane Gay

I go to school for a very long time and get some degrees and finally move to a very small town in the middle of a cornfield. I leave someone behind. I tell myself I have worked so hard I can't choose a man over a career. I want to choose the man over the career. I rent an apartment, the nicest place I've ever lived as an adult. I have a guest bathroom. I don't save lives, but I try not to ruin them.

This is the dream, everyone says—a good job, tenure track. I have an office I don't have to share with two or four people. My name is on the engraved panel just outside my door. My name is spelled correctly. I have my own printer. The luxury of this cannot be overstated. I randomly print out a document; I sigh happily as the printer spits it out, warm. I have a phone with an extension, and when people call the number they are often looking for me. There are a lot of shelves, but I like my books at home. In every movie I've ever seen about professors, there are books. I quickly unpack three boxes, detritus I accumulated in graduate school—sad drawer trash, books I'll rarely open again—but I'm a professor now. I must have books on display in my office. It is an unspoken rule.

I put a dry-erase board on my door. Old habits die hard. Every few weeks I pose a new question. What's your favorite movie? (*Pretty Woman*.) What's your favorite musical? (*West Side Story*.) What do you want for Christmas? (Peace of mind.) Currently: What is your favorite cocktail? Best answer: "Free."

The department's administrative assistant gives me the rundown on important things—mailbox, office supplies, photocopy code. I forget the code weekly. She is friendly, patient, kind, but if you cross her, there will be trouble. I vow to never cross her.

There is a mind-numbing orientation that begins with a student playing acoustic guitar. A threatening sing-along vibe fills the room. The student is not a chanteur. Most of the audience cringes visibly. I hide in the very last row. For the next two days I accumulate knowledge I will never use—math all over again.

I'll be teaching three classes, two of which I've not quite taught before. Turns out when you say you can do something, people believe you.

Ten minutes before my first class, I run to the bathroom and vomit. I'm afraid of public speaking, which makes teaching complicated.

When I walk into the classroom, the students stare at me like I'm in charge. They wait for me to say something. I stare back and wait for them to do something. It's a silent power struggle. Finally, I tell them to do things and they do those things. I realize I am, in fact, in charge. We'll be playing with Legos. For a few minutes I am awesome because I have brought toys.

Teaching three classes requires serious memorization when it comes to student names. The students tend to blur. It will take nearly three weeks for me to remember Ashley A. and Ashley M. and Matt and Matt and Mark and Mark and so on. I rely heavily on pointing. I color-code the students. *You in the green shirt. You in the orange hat.*

I get my first paycheck. We are paid once a month, which requires the kind of budgeting I am incapable of. Life is unpleasant after the twenty-third or so. I've been a graduate student for so long it's hard to fathom that one check can have four numbers and change. Then I see how much The Man takes. Damn The Man.

Students don't know what to make of me. I wear jeans and Converse. I have tattoos up and down my arms. I'm tall. I am not petite. I am the child of immigrants. Many of my students have never had a black teacher before. I can't help them with that. I'm the only black professor in my department. This will probably never change for the whole of my career, no matter where I teach. I'm used to it. I wish I weren't. There seems to be some unspoken rule about the number of academic spaces people of color can occupy at the same time. I have grown weary of being the only one.

When I was a student listening to a boring professor drone endlessly, I usually thought, *I will never be that teacher*. One day, I am delivering a lecture and realize, in that moment, I am *that* teacher. I stare out at the students, most of them not taking notes, giving me that soul-crushing dead-eye stare that tells me, *I wish I were anywhere but here.* I think, I wish I were *anywhere but here*. I talk faster and faster to put us all out of our misery. I become incoherent. Their dead-eye stares haunt me for the rest of the day, then longer.

I keep in touch with my closest friend from graduate school. We both really enjoy our new jobs, but the learning curve is steep. There is no shallow end. We dance around metaphors about drowning. During long conversations we question the choice to be proper, modern women. There is so much grading. There's a lot to be said for barefoot kitchen work when staring down a stack of research papers.

Walking down the hall, I hear a young woman saying "Dr. Gay" over and over and think, *That Dr. Gay is rather rude for ignoring the poor student*. I turn around to say something before I realize she is talking to me.

I worry some of my students don't own any clothes with zippers or buttons or other methods of closure and fastening. I see a lot of words faded and stretched across asses, bra straps, pajama pants, often ill-fitting. In the winter, when there is snow and ice outside, boys come to class in basketball shorts and flip flops. I worry about their feet, their poor little toes.

Helicopter parents e-mail me for information about their children. *How is my son doing? Is my daughter attending class?* I encourage them to open lines of communication with their children. I politely tell them there are laws preventing such communication without their child's written consent. The child rarely consents.

There is nothing new in the new town, and I know no one. The town is a flat, scarred strip of land with half-abandoned strip malls. And then there is the corn, so much of it, everywhere, stretching in every direction for miles. Most of my colleagues live fifty miles away. Most of my colleagues have families. I go north to Chicago. I go east to Indianapolis. I go south to St. Louis. I take up competitive scrabble and win the first tournament I enter. In the last round, I encounter a nemesis who gets so angry when I beat him he refuses to shake my hand and flounces out of the tournament in a huff. The sweetness of that victory lingers. The next time I see him, at another tournament, he'll point and say, "Best two out of three. Best. Two. Out. Of. Three." I best him in two out of three.

My own parents ask, *How is my daughter doing?* I offer them some version of the truth.

Sometimes, during class, I catch students staring at their cell phones beneath their desks like they're in a cone of invisibility. It's as funny as it is irritating. Sometimes, I cannot help but say, "I do see you." Other times, I confiscate their electronic devices.

Sometimes, when students are doing group work, I sneak a look at my own phone like I am in a cone of invisibility. I am part of the problem.

I try to make class fun, engaging, *experiential*. We hold a mock debate about social issues in composition. We use Twitter to learn about crafting microcontent in new media writing. We play *Jeopardy!* to learn about professional reports in professional writing. College and kindergarten aren't as different as you think. Every day, I wonder, *How do I keep these students meaningfully engaged, educated, and entertained for fifty minutes? How do I keep them from staring at me with dead eyes? How do I make them want to learn?* It's tiring. Sometimes, I think the answer to each of these questions is *I can't*.

There is a plague on grandmothers. The elder relations of my students begin passing away at an alarming rate one week. I want to warn the surviving grandmothers, somehow. I want them to live. The excuses the students come up with for absences and homework amuse me in how ludicrous and improbable they are. They think I want to know. They think I need their explanations. They think I don't know they're lying. Sometimes I simply say, "I know you are lying. You say it best when you say nothing at all."

I try not to be old. I try not to think, *When I was your age . . .* , but often, I do remember when I was their age. I enjoyed school; I loved learning and worked hard. Most of the people I went to school with did too. We partied hard, but we still showed up to class and did what we had to do. An alarming number of my students don't seem to *want* to be in college. They are in school because they don't feel they have a choice or have nothing better to do; because their parents are making them attend college; because, like most of us, they've surrendered to the rhetoric that to succeed in this country you need a college degree. They are not necessarily incorrect. And yet, all too often, I find myself wishing I could teach more students who actually want to be in school, who don't resent education being *foisted* upon them. I wish there were viable alternatives for students who would rather be anywhere but in a classroom. I wish, in all things, for a perfect world.

A number of students find my website. This is teaching in the digital age. They find my writing, much of which is, shall we say, explicit in nature. News travels fast. They want to talk to me about these things in the hall after class, in my office, out and about on campus. It's awkward and flattering but mostly awkward. They also know too much about my personal life. They know about the random guy who spent the night, who helped me kill a couple bottles of wine and made me breakfast. I have to start blogging differently.

I get along with the students. They are generally bright and charming even when they are frustrating. They make me love my job both in and out of the classroom. Students show up at my office to discuss their personal problems. I try to maintain boundaries. There are breakups with long-term boyfriends and bad dates and a lecherous professor in another department and a roommate who leaves her door open while she's getting nailed and this thing that happened at the bar on Friday and difficult decisions about whether to go to graduate school or go on the job market. Each of these situations is a crisis. I listen and try to dispense the proper advice. This is not the same advice my friends and I give to one another. What I really want to say to these students, most of them young women, is "GIRL!"

I am quite content to be in my thirties, and nothing affirms that more than being around people in their late teens and early twenties.

In grad school, we heard lurid tales of department meetings where heated words were exchanged and members of various factions almost came to blows. I was looking forward to the drama, only to learn my department meets once or twice a semester rather than every week. Instead, we meet in committees. The chairs of those committees report to the department chair. Committee meetings are not my favorite part of the job. There are politics and agendas and decades of history of which I know little and understand even less. Everyone means well, but there's a lot of bureaucracy. I prefer common sense.

The first semester ends and I receive my evaluations. Most of the students think I did a decent job, some think I did a great job, and then there are those who didn't. I assign too much work, they say. I expect too much. I don't consider these faults. A student writes, "Typical first year professor." I have no idea what that means.

Over winter break, my friend from graduate school and I have another long lamentation about choices and taking jobs in the middle of nowhere and the (relative) sacrifices academics must often make. It is tiring to constantly be told *how lucky we are.* Luck and loneliness, it would seem, are very compatible.

I go drinking with the guy I . . . go drinking with. To call it dating would be a stretch. We are a matter of convenience. I sip on a T&T and lament my evaluations. I want to be a good teacher, and most days, I think I am. I give a damn. I want students to *like* me. I am human. I am so full of want. He tells me not to worry with such authority I almost believe him. He orders me another drink and another. I hope we don't run into any of my students because I cannot pull off professorial in my current state. That's always my prayer when we go out. Because of this, we often end up in the city fifty miles up the road. At the end of the night, two very short men get into a fight. Clothing is torn. We stand in the parking lot and watch. The men's anger, the white heat of it, fascinates me. Later, after taking a cab home, I drunkenly call the man I left behind, the man who didn't follow me. "My students hate me," I say. He assures me they don't. He says that would not be possible. I say, "Everything is terrible. Everything is great." He says, "I know."

Another semester begins, three new classes. Winter settles, ice everywhere, barren plains. There are three new sets of students, different faces but similar names. *Hey you in the khaki hat. Hey you with the purple hair.*

The goal, we are told, is tenure. To that end all faculty, even first-year professors, have to compile an annual portfolio. I assemble a record of one semester's worth of work. I try to quantify my professional worth. My colleagues write letters to attest to my various accomplishments, verifying I am on such and such committee, that I participated in such and such event, that I am a valuable and contributing member of the department. I update my vita. I clip publications. I buy a neon-green three-ring binder. This is how I rage against the machine. I spend an afternoon collating and creating labels and writing about myself with equal parts humility and bravado. It's a fine balance. Later, I tell a friend, "It was like arts and crafts for adults. I went to graduate school for this."

I stop getting lost looking for the bathroom. The building is strange, with many hallways, some hidden, and an arcane numbering system that defies logic. When I leave my door open, students passing by will ask, "Where is Dr. So-and So's office?" I say, "I have no idea."

Summer, we are told, is a time for rest, relaxation, and catching up. I teach two classes. I write a novel. I return to the place I moved from, spend weeks with the man I left behind. He says, *Don't go*. I say, *Please follow*. We remain at an impasse. I return to the cornfield. There are mere weeks of summer left. They are not enough.

A new semester begins. I have new responsibilities, including chairing a committee. Ten minutes before the first class on the first day, I run to the bathroom and puke. In my classroom, I stare at another group of students whose names I will have to remember. *You in the red shirt. You with the pink shorts.* I refuse to expect less. I try to learn better, do better. I have no idea how I got to be the one at the front of the classroom, the one who gets to be in charge of things. Most of the time, I feel like the kid who gets to sit at the adult table for the first time at Thanksgiving. I'm not sure which fork to use. My feet can't reach the floor.

*

Perhaps the most difficult narrative strategy to learn or relearn for students is showing instead of telling. In personal essays, many students describe their relationships in general ways: "She is my best friend"; "We do everything together"; "He knows what I am going to say before I say it." Notice how these broad statements fail to intrigue an audience, and, moreover, fail to make us want to know more and continue to read. As a writer, how are you differentiating your friendships, your experiences, from those of the masses? What distinguishes and defines you and your story? How are you making us care?

The latter question is an important one since most people tune out speakers and writers very quickly. Our attention spans are short. Our minds are busy. Our minds wander. The cute, brooding guy sitting across the room may be much more interesting than your paper about how you and your friend are inseparable and always have been. We tune out the minister who fails to capture our attention within the first twenty seconds. Instead, we make mental lists of what we need to do today. We learn how to nod and smile perfunctorily at the unmarried aunt who insists on showing us her stack of vacation photos of European artifacts. Yes, Aunt Ruth is *showing* us the photos, and yet her narrative is a telling, a non-sequential random telling of what she saw on vacation. We are more interested in stories that *build*, with details about characters who find themselves in predicaments and writers who make us care about them and their choices. We stick around to hear how matters were resolved. We stick around because we feel something: we identify; we care; we are curious.

First-year composition student Caleb Stephens, in his essay "Assault," does much more than tell us that he has a lifelong friend. He *shows* us the origin and dynamics of the friendship. He makes the story of their friendship his own.

Assault

Caleb Stephens

I got a phone call one night after one of my football games. After my mom told me what happened, I was stunned. My best friend, Hawk, was arrested after his football game. I sat there with the phone to my ear but I wasn't listening. All I could think was, "Not Hawk. Not him."

Hawk and I met in kindergarten on the first day of school. I was sitting by myself at lunch and Hawk walked up and sat beside me. I remember being excited that someone wanted to sit with me. The first thing he said to me was, "Why is your skin brown?" Honestly, back then, I had no idea why. I just told him, "I don't know and why do you want to know?" He said, "Because I want brown skin, too." I never heard anyone say that before.

All through elementary school we stayed at each other's houses. It seemed like trouble always found us. My family lived in a two bedroom trailer out in the middle of nowhere. It was very small, the walls were paper thin, and the whole inside was very dim because of the lack of working lights in the trailer. One night we were playing on my PlayStation in my room. Out of nowhere, my step-dad yelled out my name. I walked out into the tiny living room and he was sitting in his usual spot, on the recliner with a beer in his hand. My mom was sitting across the room from him. He yelled at me again and told me to go outside and pick out a stick for a whooping right now. I said it was ten o'clock at night; it was too dark. I waited for my mom to say something, but she looked down. She finally looked up and told my step-dad that I didn't have to do that. They started to argue and I ran back to my room. *[handwritten: contrast of home setting]*

Hawk and I tried to pretend we weren't hearing anything and were just playing video games, but we couldn't ignore the sounds coming through the thin walls--things crashing and my mom and step-dad yelling. I heard rumbling and then a thump, someone falling to the ground—and then the loud voices again. I was crying because I didn't know what to do. Hawk sat there all night telling me that we were going to be all right, that it will always get better. *[handwritten: repeats @ the end]*

I felt bad because he was comforting me, but I knew that he didn't have the best home life either. His family had this nice big house on the top of this hill right on the outskirts of my hometown. I loved going there because I felt like I could get away from life. He had his own pool and trampoline and we wound jump on. At night, we stayed in this treehouse his dad built him. When we were in sixth grade, I noticed that had bruises on his face and arms. I asked him if he was all right. He just said he was fine. Hawk didn't tell me what had happened until we were in high school. His dad often set his mom off about something stupid. When his dad left his mom, she was so mad that she would beat Hawk. He said he never knew what to do so he would just lie there until she would leave him alone, until she would finally stop. I didn't know what to say.

When I hung up the phone with my mom, I just sat on my bed. I couldn't believe what she said. I thought about all the minutes and seconds Hawk helped me through. I grabbed my phone and got on Facebook. The first things I saw was a picture of him posted by the local newspaper titled, "Local Teen Arrested for Assault." I read bits and pieces of the story that my mom told me. It said the Hawk had assaulted his mother before the game. My mom had told me that the article had left out some information. It didn't say that Hawk's mom had smacked him in the face for running late to his game. The article did say that he pushed her over and broke her wrist. He ran away to the field and she called the police. They arrested him when he left the locker room after the game. I saw the word "assault" and it disgusted me. The person who wrote that article didn't know Hawk or his mom. He didn't know a single thing about what happened to us as we grew up, what pushed us down these paths. It just made Hawk out to be a monster.

After weeks of thinking about what happened, I found out that his mother dropped the charges. For some reason, nothing really happened to him. Some bail, a court hearing, and some hurt pride is what he told me. He also told me that in jail, "it was the worst feeling ever." He warned me never to get into a situation where I could be put in jail.

Both of us have challenges to overcome from our childhoods. The phone call reminded me that even though I was sitting on my bed and Hawk was sitting in prison with handcuffs, the words that he used to comfort me all those years ago was still true; we were going to be different; we were going to be all right, and it will always get better.

Strategy Tips: The Personal Narrative

1. **What is the purpose of your essay?** Modes of writing in the first person range from reflecting, self-defining, describing, observing, informing, entertaining, and persuading. Know your purpose for your assignment and write with this purpose in mind throughout the essay.

2. **What is the occasion for your piece?** Notice that we differentiate "occasion" from "subject" or "topic," although they are certainly related. "Occasion" connotes urgency. Why do you start here? Why is this day, this anecdote, this happening, this sighting, this confrontation, this conversation, this *occasion*, different from that of any other day? If your readers feel the weight of where you start in your essay, and why it is important your start here, then they will more likely be hooked. Conversely, if this is just any other day, or the same old story and occasion, then we may feel as if we have heard this tale before, and consequently "close the book." How will you establish setting and atmosphere?

3. **Do you engage your audience at the onset?** Look at your introduction. Will your audience be curious, intrigued, hooked, or, at the very least, interested to continue to read? Do you give too much away in your opening, or are you inviting your audience to discover what you have discovered along the way?

4. **What characters will you include?** Look closely at the characters you introduce in your essay. Do you do more than introduce or mention them? How are they used? What are their functions in advancing the narrative or in achieving your purpose? What and how are the interactions between the characters in your essay significant in ultimately revealing your purpose?

5. **How are you keeping your audience's attention?** What is the conflict, internal or external, in your essay? How are you maintaining a healthy narrative tension throughout the work that maintains your audience's interest? How does your narrative sequence *build*?

6. **So what happened?** Don't just tell this. *Show it!* Your sequence of events and significant, specific, concrete details are the camera we need to move past your words in order to attain understanding and feeling. The use of detailed sensory imagery—words that engage all of our senses—matter in personal writing because your words will do more than convey what you say; your reader will pick up on what you don't say, on what you now need not say, but rather on the thoughts and ideas the sensory images

evoke. Instead of just telling us how or what your felt, you *involve* your audience more in your narrative when you allow us to draw our own interpretations and conclusions by using our own senses. It's as if we, too, are at the scene, experiencing what you experienced, sensing what you sensed. As you write and strive to show concrete, sensory details, let some of these details (and not flat out telling) reveal your feelings, judgments, or ideas. Look at an example that differentiates the impact of showing versus telling.

Telling: I wondered who owned this house; it was in bad shape.

Showing: Beneath the red shutters, globs of paint, random pustules on the face of the house stone, revealed the careless, unsteady hand of its owner.

Notice the difference here between telling and showing. In the second sentence, we see the house quite vividly. Moreover, through sensory imagery, we know more about the owner. The imagery allows for interpretation, not only from the writer, but also our shared judgment of what sloppy painting may suggest. We are more curious about the person who does own the house. In other words, we are eager to want to continue to read. We are more involved as readers, seekers, interpreters. The second writer conveys the idea that the house "was in bad shape" without telling it. The house in the first sentence could describe one of many houses that are in bad shape; it is nondescript, uninteresting. Also, we are not as curious about its owner.

7. **How do your voice and tone relate to the narrative action?** How are you embracing your "I" voice? What do your voice and tone say about you and your attitude toward your subject? Are you more of an observer, or a participant? Listen closely to not only what you say, but how you say it. When embracing your "I," how do you want to be heard and subsequently envisioned by your audience—as the self-effacing college freshman who gets hiccups in the middle of internship interview, or as the nostalgic, pensive daughter searching for clues concerning her father's desertion? Your narrative voice will be analyzed by your reader and, when it is strategic and effectively in sync with proposed topic and mood, engaging and welcoming, it can greatly enhance your overall purpose.

8. **What do you leave us with?** Some of the most memorable personal essays leave us, quite simply, with something that is memorable. Your conclusion must do more than summarize what you already said. Here, you may go back to what you have foreshadowed and repeat a striking, ironic, or haunting line, as Caleb Stephens does in "Assault." Alternatively, think about ending with an image, as Roxanne Gay does in "Typical First Year Professor," that *shows* her repeated insecurity and vulnerability when a new semester commences: "I feel like the kid who gets to sit at the adult table for the first time at Thanksgiving. I'm not sure which fork to use. My feet can't reach the floor." The essay ends, but the conclusion resonates. We are still thinking and feeling. We feel as if our time invested in reading the essay was well worth it.

Personal Essay Assignment: The Self-Definition Essay

It is the first day of class and the teacher asks the students to introduce themselves. She starts with you. What do you say? How do you sum up who you are in a minute? You cannot. You tell the class where you live and how many siblings you have and your college major—you think. The teacher moves on to the next student. His list is basically the same, but he lives somewhere else, he is an only child, and he has an undecided major. After the third student you stop listening. All you hear is blah blah blah, the same old things, lots of telling—until Chase asks the teacher if he can show the class a photo of Ruff, his greyhound. The teacher agrees, and Chase proceeds to explain how he saved Ruff's life by giving him CPR. He lay Ruff on is right side, checked his femoral artery for a pulse, opened his airway, gave five rescue breaths into his nose, braced the dog against his body, put his thumb under Ruff's armpit, and started compressions. He didn't have to state his major. You said, "So you want to be a vet?"

Since you cannot define yourself fully in one minute, or even in one essay, then why, when writing a self-definition essay, would you spread yourself too thin by delivering a non-sequential list of all of your interests and traits, a type of telling? You will find it quite difficult to sustain your audience's attention that way. Instead, *focus on one major personality trait or interest* that you have, and *show* us who you are. So, for this assignment, reintroduce yourself to your classmates, your audience. **In an essay of at least three pages, think about the various ways you define yourself, and *narrow your topic* to create and *build* a narrative that *shows* you, or best reflects who you are.** Think about the narrative strategies listed above and incorporate these strategies in your essay. Before you write your essay, here are two student self-definition essays written by college freshmen during their first semester. Look closely at how first year-college composition students Joe McKernan and Hollie Imperato employ repeated themes, sensory imagery, a forward, focused sequence, and, moreover, how they show instead of just tell. Look at their concluding sentences. What do they leave you with?

A Bloody Nose and the Art of Empathy

Joe McKernan

It was a cold, January morning in the suburbs of Philadelphia. My watch read six-thirty by the time I ran out to my car wearing my jacket and scrubs, the piercing wind going straight through my pants. I wished they made scrubs for the wintertime. Getting in my car, I immediately blasted the heat and put on my favorite feature, the seat warmer. Before I began my trip to Chester County Hospital, I put on my ChapStick, as the cold, dry weather shriveled my lips into a painful sandpaper-like state. Turning on my headlights, I began the drive.

Still smelling of chlorine from the previous night's swim practice, my muscles ached and my eyelids were heavy. In my mind, I was reviewing facts about the Constitution's Amendments and the life cycle of a cell, since those were the tests I had later in the day. Before taking those tests, however, I would shadow the nurses at the hospital. It was my fifth month doing this, and my third day in the pediatric unit. I considered skipping to just study more, since there was probably not much else to see, but in the end, I decided not to do that.

Arriving in the parking lot, I made my way to the parking garage. I drove around and around in circles to get to the roof of the garage, driving past many empty spots on my journey to the roof. I did not understand why they forced our class to park on the roof, but, I did not make the rules. I stepped out of my car and walked to the bus stop where the bus picks people up and drives them to the drop off station at the hospital entrance. Trying to hide my face from the wind, I stood waiting ten minutes for the bus. Once I arrived at the entrance, I walked to the area where the other students and I were to sign in, but there was no sign of my teacher. We waited another ten minutes for her arrival. I thought of all the lost time I could have used for studying.

Once I signed in, I made my way to the pediatric department. I tried to predict what I would witness today. Would I watch children receive breakfast and take medicine? Will the nurses show me equipment while the kids sleep? Or, will I get to watch the nurses do their charting? I looked at the time as I prepared myself for what was sure to be a long hour and a half. But then I thought, maybe the ten-year-old boy with sickle cell anemia would still be there. We had spent some time together talking about the Eagles and were both excited about the Super Bowl in February. He asked me if the Eagles won, would I go to the parade? I told him, "Yes, my mom doesn't want me to go, but my dad said he would convince her that I should." I winked at him and he looked at me with a smile and an admiring gaze. He told me he was in the hospital for a sickle cell crisis and his stomach, elbows and knees hurt a lot because his blood cells were the wrong shape. It made him mad that he had to be in the hospital, because he couldn't do what he wanted and there were only girls around. He tried to act tough, but his eyes told a different story; they showed his emotions. He was angry and fearful. I looked around his room and tried to see what he saw. There was his bed, a bedside table, a television with cartoons on, some games and books, but no one to play with him. The nurses came and went quickly, checking his vital signs, saying a few kind words. It was busy on the unit. I was glad I was able to visit with him. He seemed to like it.

As I walked through the double doors of the department, a nurse spotted me and called, "Joe! I am so glad you are here! We need you right away!" I had no time to take my jacket off as I rushed to see why they could possibly need me. When I walked in, I saw my ten-year-old friend. He was screaming and fighting as the nurses tried to draw blood from him. The nurse who called my name told me to hold his hand and talk with him. She said that he was in the stage of life where he did not like girls at all and only would listen to boys. I held his hand and talked to him in an attempt to calm him down, but it was not working. Then, I felt a rush of moisture from my nose. I touched it and blood covered my hand. I had a bloody nose! I could not remember the last time I had a bloody nose. When the boy noticed my grabbing for a tissue to stop the bleeding, he broke out in laughter and his eyes danced with amusement. He thought it was the funniest thing. While he was distracted by my bleeding, the nurses took his blood with no problem. The boy and I laughed over it as the nurses finished their duties. I stayed with him the rest of my time on the unit and we talked sports and played a game. What I thought was going to be a long hour and a half flew by too quickly. I wished I could stay longer. My young friend was happy and I said goodbye.

As I left the hospital that day I thought how strange it was that I had a bloody nose. I knew God worked in mysterious ways, but this was definitely a surprise. I signed out of the hospital and stepped outside to wait for the bus. My chapped lips cracked as I broke a smile, and I no longer felt the cold.

Hearing in Colors

Hollie Imperato

I did not always hear this way. I used to hear music for its dancing notes and light rhythms that kept my foot tapping. I would hear Frank Sinatra's voice through my pink CD player and dance across the cracked tile of my kitchen floor. My brother never danced with me because he was too busy with his Legos, but I only had to wait a few years until there were two little girls for my mom to yell at about dancing on the tile while wearing socks. Apparently, you can slip and get hurt. And apparently it's true, because I did. But that didn't stop my little sister and me from twirling across the floor; we just took our socks off the next time.

Gracie came into my life from China when I was five years old. As we grew up, we took turns using the TV remote, I taught her how to ride a bike, and we would push Sneakers into the tub or cut off all his whiskers; the poor cat only survived because my brother came to his rescue. We would take trips to Claire's and buy matching earrings with our allowance and play connect the dots with stars. We would even invite Noah along on our outdoor adventures (which was technically against the rules because he was a boy, but we figured we could make an exception considering he was our brother). The combination of her dark brown eyes, smooth skin and jet-black hair was a striking image of beauty, and her heart was kind. On Valentine's Day she would make me Dora themed cards and handpick daisies from our front yard. She shared her school supplies with a student that couldn't afford them. She taught me just as much as I taught her, and because of that my youth was full of yellow from the flowers on the forsythia bush, purple laughter and red from silk dresses.

Nine years of blissful childhood passed and my double-digit birthday was around the corner. Three days before my birthday, we spent the afternoon caged in the living room due to the seemingly everlasting rain. The next day, we had planned to take a drive on back roads through the last oranges and reds of fall, but Grace came down with the flu; we were stuck in the house for the day again. That night Grace's flu worsened until the doctors determined that they lied and it was not actually the flu. By the morning of my birthday, Gracie's soul floated into heavenly lights, taking all my colors with her.

Grieving is a process. People say that it's different for everyone, yet they commonly say "I understand how you feel." These words hit me hard at first, but eventually my eyes glazed over each time they were said. I went to a support group, and they seemed to understand how I felt. I went to therapy, and they supposedly knew how I felt because they went to college for it. And my friends understood too, because they had dogs or cats that died a couple years ago. Each time someone "understood," it only confused me more because they didn't. How could an abundance of people understand the feelings that I could not even comprehend myself? They didn't know that I couldn't get out of bed when the rest of my family could. How could they? They didn't know that Grace and I would share a chocolate cupcake on Chinese New Year because we thought the traditional mooncakes were gross. They didn't know what it felt like to see a younger family member die before she got the chance to turn ten like I did, or how alone I felt afterwards. I knew, though. So when they said they understood, I was confused as to how they could because for me, depression was too hard to comprehend.

Depression is a dishonest grey— and not just things you can see. It is dishonest because your favorite cinnamon roll suddenly tastes like all the others, but you know it should taste differently. The smell of your favorite blanket becomes empty and meaningless, but you know it's your favorite because your mom made it for you. Depression tells lies about things you love, and it feels like it will always be that way, like you're eternally cemented in a stick-figure drawing. It felt as though my family was on the other side of the paper, and my short stick-arms could not reach out to them.

Based on my dad's standards, a stick-figure drawing is pretty darn good, but I wanted more than grey straight lines. My dad understood and bought me my first drawing pad. It had a simple brown cover and black spiral binding at the top. It wasn't anything exciting but I thought I would give it a shot. I took my Hello Kitty pencil and started to draw something. I can't remember what I drew first, but I remember where it ended up— crumpled up on the tired creme carpet in my room. That was enough effort for the week, but the following week I started another drawing and that one had the same fate as the last. Noah decided to boost my confidence in my ability by looking at all my failed masterpieces and laughing. This put a bump in my motivation to try again, but after a few days of staring mindlessly in bed, I picked up the pencil and made another attempt.

For the first time in a while, I was trying at something. It went from drawing every week to drawing a few times a week, and then eventually I was drawing every day. The discipline of learning to draw spilled into other areas of my life; I even started doing my homework. One day, I used this momentum to lift my apprehensive hand and reached for my pink CD player. Having laid in dusty silence since the last time I used it, Sinatra's voice came booming through the speakers, filling my room and startling my parents. I heard soothing green and blue waves. I heard Gracie's rolling, purple laughter and my mom's red, foreboding voice about the socks on our feet; I heard all the colors I thought I had lost. I listened to the colors, grabbed my pencil and put my feelings to paper. When I was done, I created a painful and honest depiction of my mind. I felt better. The drawing was good. It was still stuck in grey but maybe it was beautiful.

I was good at art when I created it honestly and it continued to get better during the couple weeks I was home from school. I would put music on that told the truth and I would draw the darkness from my mind out onto a lonely sheet of paper. The most inspiring and sincere music was Steven Curtis Chapman's album, *Beauty Will Rise*. I heard all the colors I was feeling in every song and it was nice to know that I wasn't feeling them alone. There were songs that were red and upsetting that made me ask questions in my art, but some songs were spring pink. The more I listened to his voice the more I drew and wanted to try. I didn't see the harm in trying paint either, so I did that too and soon enough I was using blue to paint the overfilled ocean I felt. Art became my outlet; my beautifully honest paintings were the product of hearing in colors, and eventually I found healing from it.

Now, my colors have returned for me to use. My mind is no longer trapped in the two dimensional, misunderstood world it was in for so long. I would say that I lament my time in grey, but depression gave me the gift to hear colors and paint them as feelings. As I navigate new experiences like college and life's unexpectancies, my hello kitty pencil and simple drawing pad will always understand how I feel, and the colors I use can never be taken from the page. God does not use easy experiences to enrich people and their gifts but rather he uses our fury filled fists and the red from the angry questions we often yell at him to show us he is faithful. For every white fury and angry red that comes with falling in my life, I have a gift to use that reminds me to take my socks off so that I don't slip again.

In-Class Exercise: Peer Review

In a full class or small group workshop, critique several of your peers' self-definition essays and provide useful, concrete feedback concerning what is working well and want needs to be reconsidered and revised. As you prepare to provide feedback, determine whether the writer has fulfilled the purpose of the assignment; established a sense of "occasion," setting, and atmosphere; engaged you at the onset; created three-dimensional characters; sustained your interest through rising tension, conflict, and/or plot sequence; and left you thinking with resonating words or images. Also, does the writing show more than tell? How does the narrative voice add to the meaning and purpose of the essay?

Additional Assignment

After receiving comments from your instructor and from your peers, revise your self-definition essay. Revising requires more thought than editing. When you edit, you proofread for errors in grammar, spelling, and punctuation. When you think about it, revising, literally, means "re-vision" or "seeing again." It requires a total reevaluation of your essay's organization, purpose, and effect on your audience. Address the strength of your ideas, your support, your diction (exact word choice), your narrative voice, and your sentence fluency. To what central idea does your essay build? Have you successfully conveyed that central idea or feeling to your audience?

Chapter [7]

Second-Person Point of View

© MK photograp55/Shutterstock.com

Unlearning

The second person point of view should never be used in writing. It draws too much attention to itself and is more of a novelty or "flash" than an effective perspective serving the purpose of an essay or narrative.

Relearning

While it is true that second person point view is not the preferred perspective in many types of formal, academic essays due to its informal tone, the second-person perspective often is advantageous in instructional, business, technical, and fiction writing.

Just like tense, a consistent point of view is important throughout your paper. If you are writing a paper that is centered on you as a writer, then you will likely have a composition written in first-person point of view, using singular pronouns such as "I" and "me" as well as plural pronouns such as "we" and "our." When it comes to second-person writing and second-person point of view, writers consistently will use the following singular and plural pronouns:

Second Person Pronouns	
Singular	you; your; yours; yourself
Plural	you; your; yours; yourselves

While the second-person perspective is not ideal in many types of formal writing, it does have a place in workplace writing. For instance, second-person point of view is known as the "you" view or "you" attitude in business and technical writing. Both business and technical writing require more emphasis on those who read the written material than the person who wrote it. Furthermore, both business and technical writing allow writers to break with consistency and write using an acceptable mix of first, second, and third person. Take a look at the following sample email:

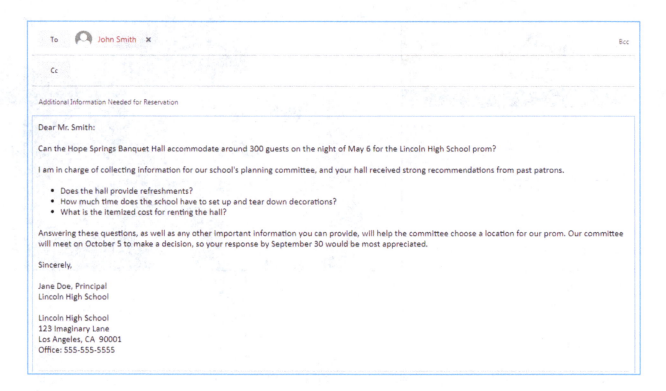

As you can see, the sample email demonstrates an acceptable mix of first-, second-, and third-person writing. The first-person writing addresses information regarding the sender, Jane Doe. The second-person writing addresses information regarding the receiver, Mr. Smith. Finally, the third-person writing addresses information regarding the topic, the prom. While using a combination of first, second, and third person is entirely acceptable for a professional correspondence, this type of writing should not occur in a formal academic paper.

Instructional Writing

One of the more obvious examples of using second person is in instructional writing. This textbook, for instance, is an example of instructional writing; you likely noticed the second-person perspective throughout. First-person usage in instructional writing is permitted but also highly restricted in favor of the more appropriate second person. However, there is more to instructional writing than the second-person perspective.

Second-person instructional writing incorporates the imperative mood, a form of verb that makes a direct command or request. The following chart provides some examples of the imperative mood:

Imperative Mood (Examples)
Touch the screen for more information. *Read* the following passage. *Go* to the back of the book for the answers.

As you can see, examples like the ones above make a command. Notice how the second-person perspective is implied instead of stated (*you* touch, *you* read, *you* go). This textbook, when utilizing the second-person perspective, makes requests, suggestions, and commands from time to time, demonstrating the use of the imperative mood.

Business Writing

It is easy to imagine why second-person writing has an important role in business writing. On one hand, businesses communicate with consumers in order to persuade them to purchase the product they are selling. Readers appreciate when the information conveyed is for or about them, as well as a business or advertiser's attempt to look at information from their (the audience or consumer) perspective.

© Pressmaster/Shutterstock.com

Employees of a particular business also regularly communicate internally with each other or externally to employees of other businesses via second-person memos, emails, or formal letters. The use of second person provides direct, often specific instruction and information that the receivers of these communications appreciate. Compare the following example:

FIRST PERSON: We are asking all employees to complete the attached questionnaire regarding work hours.

SECOND PERSON: Because your voice matters, please complete the attached questionnaire regarding your work hours.

As you can see, there is more of a focus on the reader when written in second person rather than the first person. There is less distance between the sender and receiver in the second-person example than with the first-person example. Also, saying "your voice matters" conveys positive feelings toward the reader. Therefore, second-person writing is able to accomplish a lot more than first-person writing, especially in business communication.

Technical Writing

Technical communication and business communication both deal with writing in the workplace setting. However, technical writing has a specific focus of helping workers make decisions, complete tasks, and receive answers to questions. This type of writing usually manifests in the form of a memo, email, various forms of letters, short and long reports, and proposals.

One of the similarities between technical and academic writing is the importance stressed on the writer to analyze audience. With technical writing, the focus is specifically on the audience's interest and goals in regards to reading something. The reader is the subject, and that's why second person is so important in technical writing (because it is reader-focused). The following email provides an example of reader-focused writing:

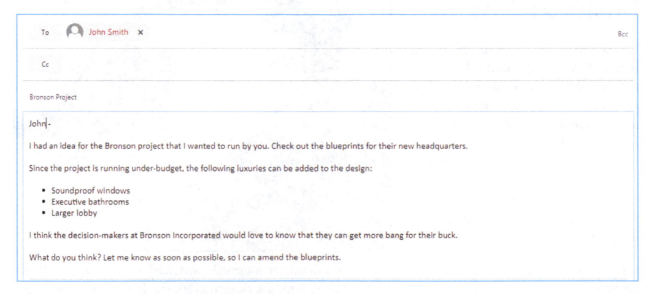

As you can see, the email is centered on the reader, who has to make a decision as to what to do with the extra monies available for a building project. This is a stark contrast from academic writing, where the reader usually is not the subject.

Fiction Writing

Often, the second point of view is used in advertising either directly (Burger King's "Have it your way") or implied (Nike's "Just do it"). Marketers use this point of view because it resonates as personal, as if they are speaking directly to a viewer or reader and addressing that individual's specific wants or needs. The imperative tone also commands the attention of a marketer's audience.

In fiction, the second-person point of view also actively, immediately, involves the reader. Look at the opening lines of Mari Ness' short story, "Inhabiting Your Skin" (*Apex Magazine*, June 2, 2015, https://apex-magazine.com/inhabiting-your-skin/).

> The house won't stop talking to you. You've tried to turn it off, several times, but it keeps happily turning itself back on, with a little chirp and a hum. You've tried to lower the volume, which works for a little bit, until the house gets frustrated, and suddenly shrieks out at high pitch, overriding its controls, "ARE YOU LISTENING TO ME?" You get worried about the neighbors.

Notice how, at once, you are pulled into the narrative. The second-person point of view allows, for the reader, instant involvement, as if we are in the mind and thoughts of the characters, or, in many cases, the reader becomes a character, immersing the reader even deeper into the narrative. Most often, second-person short stories are written in the present tense since the present tense also generates a sense of urgency and intimacy. While second-person narration is not used in fiction as often as first or third person, it can be an effective perspective if you have a planned purpose for including or "dragging" your reader more directly into the familiarity of the narrative and its characters.

Practice Exercises

1. Write a "how to" instruction manual using the second-person point of view. For example, you may want to describe how to throw a perfect curveball, how to sell goods on eBay, or how to make a lemon meringue pie. Make sure your language is clear and your sequence is easy to understand. Put yourself in the place of your audience, individuals who may have little to no knowledge of your subject matter. Use as few words as necessary to get your point across. When you are done, ask someone to follow your instructions to make sure there are no gaps or misunderstandings in the directions.

2. Write a short-short story (fiction) of approximately 500 to 1,000 words using second-person narration. Focus on one or two characters, one conflict, one or two scenes, one central image, and precise nouns and verbs in order to avoid unnecessary adjectives and adverbs. For example, instead of writing the dog "jumped quickly," say the dog "pounced." Say "armoire" instead of the "innate moveable cabinet." Because of your word limit, keep your central idea and focus narrow in order to more thoroughly explore the fundamental elements of short-short story writing that will generate reader interest and feeling.

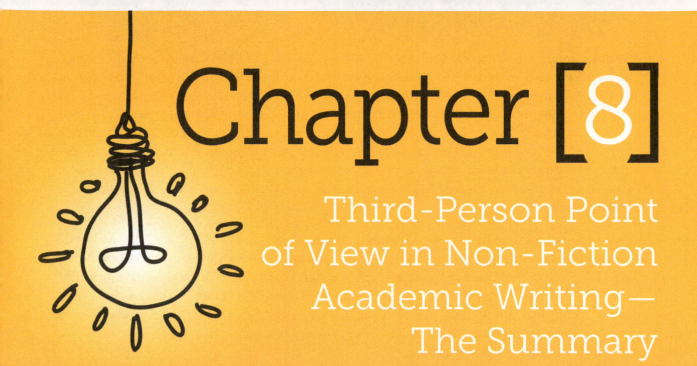

Chapter [8]

Third-Person Point of View in Non-Fiction Academic Writing— The Summary

Unlearning

In academic writing, the third-person point of view hinders personal observations or viewpoints.

Relearning

In academic writing, the third-person point of view rings more objective than the first-person point of view, as if the discoveries and observations chronicled by the narrator have been made by a seemingly impartial, neutral recorder.

For example, you have been asked to critique an essay concerning environmental sustainability. You are a student who has little interest in the topic, but you are forced to write the essay in order to earn a decent grade and pass the class. In essence, you are a dispassionate recorder of your thoughts and observations as you read. You use the third-person point of view to document, or show, a blatant contradiction you observe in the essay: "While the intent of the author, a corporate president, is commendable in documenting the deleterious impact of carbon emissions, he lists twelve other cities he will fly to in the company jet in the next few months on his university speaking tour to discuss the impact of carbon emissions on the environment."

This is *your* observation. You know that airplanes release many pounds of carbon dioxide per mile traveled. You espouse your observation, your viewpoint, by showing the contradiction and by using third-person perspective ("he"). By using textual support and distancing yourself from the facts through the use of third person, your observations resonate as objective. Had you shifted the point of view to first person and said, "I think this guy is just another greedy corporate hypocrite," your audience may pick up on a underlying bias that puts unwanted focus on you and detracts from the valid textual incongruity you have shown. In academic critiques and arguments, third-person narration is ideal in presenting, more objectively, information, subject matter, observations, and arguments. The focus remains on the subject rather than on the subjective reader/writer/responder.

Third-person pronouns include the singular, subjective case personal pronouns "he" "she," "it," and "one" and the plural, subjective case personal pronoun "they"; the objective case singular personal pronouns "him," "her," "it," and "one" and the plural objective case personal pronoun "them"; the possessive pronouns "his," "her," and "theirs"; and the intensive or reflexive pronouns "himself," "herself," "itself," "oneself," and "themselves." In formal academic writing, when you critique, argue, and persuade, the use of these pronouns via the third-person point of view can be an effective way to present your observations and perspective in a relatively credible, seemingly unbiased manner.

In this textbook, we will focus on three types of third-person academic writing: the summary (Chapter 8), the critique (Chapter 9), and the argument (Chapter 11). For the summary, the focus should be exclusively on the subject, and not on you.

THE SUMMARY

Unlearning

Writing summaries basically involves using a thesaurus to find synonyms and changing words around. Two valid summaries can be completely different depending on the details the writers choose to include.

Relearning

Good summaries necessitate good reading comprehension. Simply rearranging words will not guarantee an accurate interpretation of the author's main points. In addition, not all words or sentences need to be restated. A summary, by definition, is a condensed version of the original passage. When writing the summary, emphasize what the author of the original passage emphasizes. Good summaries include significant details and minimize or exclude trivial, insignificant details.

Your job, when writing a fair and thorough summary, is to follow the author's lead in both content and tone. Never should you include information that does not appear in the original passage; nor should we hear a voice or tone that does not match that of the author. Here, with the summary, the third-person perspective and neutrality are paramount to success.

So what exactly is a summary? A summary is your restatement of the key, emphasized ideas and sections of thought in an essay. As you closely read an essay, you will notice that certain words and themes are repeated, and for a reason. These words and themes comprise an author's main points. You must include these main points in your summary. If you don't follow an author's emphasis and order, your audience will question the validity of your summary and, moreover, your reading comprehension.

First and foremost, you must fully comprehend what you read before you can accurately and fairly summarize it. How can you legitimately summarize an essay you don't understand? Reading comprehension requires time and effort: rereading; dividing the essay into separate, dominant theme segments; circling repeated key words; and finally, expressing the author's train of thought in terms of *prominence and sequence*. In essence, highlight and emphasize what the author emphasizes, and follow the author's order of presentation.

Strategy Tips: Writing the Summary

1. Read the essay carefully in its entirety. When you are finished, ask yourself what the author's main idea is and see if you can locate this main idea, or thesis, in the essay.

2. Reread the essay, this time breaking down the essay into paragraph divisions, each division representing a distinct theme or unit of thought that contributes to the whole—the author's main idea. Look for repeated words and themes that link opening paragraphs together. When the author moves to another unit of thought, then identify this second section by bracketing these similarly themed paragraphs together. In essence, you are breaking down the essay into its major divisions, and what is emphasized in each division must be represented in your summary.

3. Ask yourself what the author emphasizes. What information is significant and must be included in the essay, and what information is less significant? Often, the author will give you clues as to what is important and what is inconsequential. Highlight or circle key words and sentences.

4. Start writing. Be sure to identify the name of the essay (in quotation marks) and its author at the onset when you restate the author's main idea, a statement that will serve as your summary thesis. Remember, when you summarize, use your own words throughout the essay. Since your purpose in the summary is to restate the author's main ideas, never should we hear you, your viewpoints, or your opinions, in the summary. Use the third-person perspective in order to be as objective as possible when echoing not only the author's content but also the author's point of view or tone. Also, do not quote the author. Again, a summary is a restatement of the author's key points *in your own words*.

5. Summarize each of the paragraph divisions in a few sentences. Combine your section summaries with your thesis statement, this time including effective transitions between the different section summaries. Match your words with the author's words, making sure that you are fairly and accurately reiterating what the author says in both content and tone. Look at what you have emphasized in the summary; you may add more sentences if necessary to comprehensively echo what the author has emphasized.

6. Reread and proofread your summary to make sure that, proportionally, you give equal weight to the emphasized points in the original passage, and that your sentences are concise, precise, and clear.

Summary Practice

After you carefully read Virginia Postrel's "Yes, Don't Impede Medical Progress," reread the essay again, this time referring to the summary strategy tips. Where is her thesis? Where in the essay does Postrel switch gears? Identify the essay's major divisions and lump together or bracket the paragraphs that comprise each unit of thought that contributes to the central idea or theme. Highlight, circle, or underline repeated, emphasized words and ideas.

Yes, Don't Impede Medical Progress

Virginia Postrel
THE WALL STREET JOURNAL , DECEMBER 05, 2001

To many biologists, the recently announced creation of a cloned human embryo was no big deal. True, researchers at Advanced Cell Technology replaced the nucleus of a human egg with the genetic material of another person. And they got that cloned cell to start replicating. But their results were modest. It took 71 eggs to produce a single success, and in the best case, the embryo grew to only six cells before dying. That's not a revolution. It's an incremental step in understanding how early-stage cells develop.

And it's far from the 100 or so cells in a blastocyst, the hollow ball from which stem cells can be isolated. Scientists hope to coax embryonic stem cells into becoming specialized tissues such as nerve, muscle, or pancreatic islet cells. Therapeutic cloning, or nucleus transplantation, could make such treatments more effective.

In theory, it would work like this: Suppose I need new heart tissue or some insulin-secreting islet cells to counteract diabetes. You could take the nucleus from one of my cells, stick it in an egg cell from which the nucleus had been removed, let that develop into stem cells, and then trigger the stem cells to form the specific tissue needed. The new "cloned" tissue would be genetically mine and would not face rejection problems. It would function in my body as if it had grown there naturally, so I wouldn't face a lifetime of immunosuppressant drugs.

But all of that is a long way off. ACT and others in the field are still doing very basic research, not developing clinical therapies. Indeed, because of the difficulty of obtaining eggs, therapeutic cloning may ultimately prove impractical for clinical treatments. It could be more important as a technique for understanding cell development or studying the mutations that lead to cancer. We simply don't know right now. Science is about exploring the unknown and cannot offer guarantees.

Politics, however, feeds on fear, uncertainty, and doubt, and the word "cloning" arouses those emotions. While its scientific importance remains to be seen, ACT's announcement has rekindled the campaign to criminalize nucleus transplantation and any therapies derived from that process. Under a bill passed by the House and endorsed by the president, scientists who transfer a human nucleus into an egg cell would be subject to 10-year federal prison sentences and $1 million fines. So would anyone who imports therapies developed through such research in countries where it is legal, such as Britain. The bill represents an unprecedented attempt to criminalize basic biomedical research.

The legislation's backers consider the fear of cloning their best hope for stopping medical research that might lead to gene-level therapies. Opponents make three basic arguments for banning therapeutic cloning.

The first is that a fertilized egg is a person, entitled to full human rights. Taking stem cells out of a blastocyst is, in this view, no different from cutting the heart out of a baby. Hence, we hear fears of "embryo farming" for "spare parts."

This view treats microscopic cells with no past or present consciousness, no organs or tissues, as people. A vocal minority of Americans, of course, do find compelling the argument that a fertilized egg is someone who deserves protection from harm. That view animates the anti-abortion movement and exercises considerable influence in Republican politics.

But most Americans don't believe we should sacrifice the lives and well being of actual people to save cells. Human identity must rest on something more compelling than the right string of proteins in a petri dish, detectable only with high-tech equipment. We will never get a moral consensus that a single cell, or a clump of 100 cells, is a human being. That definition defies moral sense, rational argument, and several major religious traditions.

So cloning opponents add a second argument. If we allow therapeutic cloning, they say, some unscrupulous person will pretend to be doing cellular research but instead implant a cloned embryo in a woman's womb and produce a baby. At the current stage of knowledge, using cloning to conceive a child would indeed be dangerous and unethical, with a high risk of serious birth defects. Anyone who cloned a baby today would rightly face, at the very least, the potential of an enormous malpractice judgment. There are good arguments for establishing a temporary moratorium on reproductive cloning.

But the small possibility of reproductive cloning does not justify making nucleus transfer a crime. Almost any science might conceivably be turned to evil purposes. This particular misuse is neither especially likely—cell biology labs are not set up to deliver fertility treatments—nor, in the long run, especially threatening.

Contrary to a lot of scary rhetoric, a healthy cloned infant would not be a moral nightmare, merely the not-quite-identical twin of an older person. (The fetal environment and egg cytoplasm create some genetic variations.) Certainly, some parents might have such a baby for bad reasons, to gratify their egos or to "replace" a child who died. But parents have been having children for bad reasons since time immemorial.

Just as likely, cloned babies would be the cherished children of couples who could not have biological offspring any other way. These children might bear an uncanny resemblance to their biological parents, but that, too, is not unprecedented. Like the "test tube babies" born of in vitro fertilization, cloned children need not be identifiable, much less freaks or outcasts.

Why worry so much about a few babies? Because, say opponents, even a single cloned infant puts us on the road to genetic dystopia, a combination of Brave New World and Nazi Germany. A cloned child's genetic makeup is too well known, goes the argument, and therefore transforms random reproduction into "manufacturing" that robs the child of his autonomy. This is where the attack broadens from nucleus transfer to human genetic engineering more generally. An anti-therapeutic cloning petition, circulated by the unlikely duo of conservative publisher William Kristol and arch-technophobe Jeremy Rifkin, concludes, "We are mindful of the tragic history of social eugenics movements in the first half of the 20th century, and are united in our opposition to any use of biotechnology for a commercial eugenics movement in the 21st century."

But the "eugenics" they attack has nothing to do with state-sponsored mass murder or forced sterilization. To the contrary, they are the ones who want the state to dictate the most private aspects of family life. They are the ones who want central authorities, rather than the choices of families and individuals, to determine our genetic future. They are the ones who demand that the government control the means of reproduction. They are the ones who measure the worth of human beings by the circumstances of their conception and the purity of their genetic makeup. They are the ones who say "natural" genes are the mark of true humanity.

Winners in the genetic lottery themselves, blessed with good health and unusual intelligence, they seek to deny future parents the chance to give their children an equally promising genetic start. In a despicable moral equivalency, they equate loving parents with Nazis.

Biomedicine does have the potential to alter the human experience. Indeed, it already has. Life expectancy has doubled worldwide in the past century. Childbirth is no longer a peril to mother and infant. Childhood is no longer a time for early death. The pervasive sense of mortality that down through the ages shaped art, religion, and culture has waned.

Our lives are different from our ancestors' in fundamental ways. We rarely remark on the change, however, because it occurred incrementally. That's how culture evolves and how science works. We should let the process continue.

The Summary Annotation

Now, practice by annotating Postrel's text, a good way to prepare for your written summary. This demonstration should make your job easier and your summary a true, condensed representation of the original passage. Notice that the paragraphs are divided into six separate units of thought that ultimately contribute to the whole.

Yes, Don't Impede Medical Progress

Virginia Postrel
THE WALL STREET JOURNAL , DECEMBER 05, 2001

To many biologists, the recently announced creation of a cloned human embryo was **no big deal**. True, researchers at Advanced Cell Technology replaced the nucleus of a human egg with the genetic material of another person. And they got that cloned cell to start replicating. **But their results were modest. It took 71 eggs to produce a single success, and in the best case, the embryo grew to only six cells before dying. That's not a revolution.** It's an **incremental** step in understanding how early-stage cells develop.

And it's far from the 100 or so cells in a blastocyst, the hollow ball from which stem cells can be isolated. Scientists hope to coax embryonic stem cells into becoming specialized tissues such as nerve, muscle, or pancreatic islet cells. Therapeutic cloning, or nucleus transplantation, could make such treatments more effective.

The words in bold print reveal Postrel's repeated theme: the results at this point were "no big deal," "modest," "not a revolution." She deemphasizes that announcement of the cloned human embryo creation. In your summary, follow Postrel's lead. Do not emphasize the announcement per se.

Postrel does emphasize scientific "exploring" (see highlighted words in this section). Her thesis, although implicit in these opening paragraphs, may be gleaned from this repeated theme of "incremental" learning and discovery that may actually lead to something promising not only in theory, but in practice.

In theory, it would work like this: Suppose I need new heart tissue or some insulin-secreting islet cells to counteract diabetes. You could take the nucleus from one of my cells, stick it in an egg cell from which the nucleus had been removed, let that develop into stem cells, and then trigger the stem cells to form the specific tissue needed. The new "cloned" tissue would be genetically mine and would not face rejection problems. It would function in my body as if it had grown there naturally, so I wouldn't face a lifetime of immunosuppressant drugs.

But all of that is a long way off. ACT and others in the field are still doing **very basic research**, not developing clinical therapies. Indeed, because of the difficulty of obtaining eggs, therapeutic cloning may ultimately prove impractical for clinical treatments. It could be more important as a technique for understanding cell development or studying the mutations that lead to cancer. We **simply don't know right now**. Science is about exploring the unknown and cannot offer guarantees.

Politics, however, feeds on fear, uncertainty, and doubt, and the word "cloning" arouses those emotions. While its scientific importance remains to be seen, ACT's announcement has rekindled **the campaign to criminalize nucleus transplantation** and any therapies derived from that process. Under a bill passed by the House and endorsed by the president, scientists who transfer a human nucleus into an egg cell would be subject to 10-year federal prison sentences and $1 million fines. So would anyone who imports therapies developed through such research in countries where it is legal, such as Britain. **The bill represents an unprecedented attempt to criminalize basic biomedical research.**

The legislation's backers consider the fear of cloning their best hope for stopping medical research that might lead to gene-level therapies. Opponents make three basic arguments for banning therapeutic cloning.

The first is that a fertilized egg is a person, entitled to full human rights. Taking stem cells out of a blastocyst is, in this view, no different from cutting the heart out of a baby. Hence, we hear **fears of "embryo farming" for "spare parts."**

This view treats microscopic cells with no past or present consciousness, no organs or tissues, as people. A vocal minority of Americans, of course, do find compelling the argument that a fertilized egg is someone who deserves **protection from harm**. That view animates the anti-abortion movement and exercises considerable influence in Republican politics.

But most Americans don't believe we should sacrifice the lives and well being of actual people to save cells. Human identity must rest on something more compelling than the right string of proteins in a petri dish, detectable only with high-tech equipment. We will never get a moral consensus that a single cell, or a clump of 100 cells, is a human being. That definition defies moral sense, rational argument, and several major religious traditions.

So cloning opponents add a second argument. If we allow therapeutic cloning, they say, some unscrupulous person will pretend to be doing cellular research but instead implant a cloned embryo in a woman's womb and produce a baby. At the current stage of knowledge, using cloning to conceive a child would indeed be **dangerous and unethical, with a high risk of serious birth defects**. Anyone who cloned a baby today would rightly face, at the very least, the potential of an **enormous malpractice judgment**. There are good arguments for establishing a temporary moratorium on reproductive cloning.

Again, notice the repeated , stressed themes in bold print in this section—on the one hand, "politics," "bill," "legislation," and, tied with these, "fear, uncertainty, and doubt."

This sentence resonates as "more important" or emphasized information that you should include in your summary.

This first of three "fear" arguments for ceasing cloning research must be included in your summary, for it comprises a complete thematic unit in the essay.

The repeated fear theme is again marked by bold print.

The highlighted sentences in this paragraph represent the counterargument, or Postrel's refutation of the "fertilized egg is a person" argument, and reveal her point of view and tone. These must be included in the summary.

The second "fear" argument must also be restated in your summary, since it comprises, in argument and refutation, seven paragraphs of the essay.

Again, the words in bold emphasize the fear and legal arguments.

But the small possibility of reproductive cloning does not justify making nucleus transfer a crime. Almost any science might conceivably be turned to evil purposes. This particular misuse is neither especially likely—cell biology labs are not set up to deliver fertility treatments—nor, in the long run, especially threatening.

Contrary to a lot of scary rhetoric, a healthy cloned infant would not be a moral nightmare, merely the not-quite-identical twin of an older person. (The fetal environment and egg cytoplasm create some genetic variations.) Certainly, some parents might have such a baby for bad reasons, to gratify their egos or to "replace" a child who died. But parents have been having children for bad reasons since time immemorial.

Just as likely, cloned babies would be the cherished children of couples who could not have biological offspring any other way. These children might bear an uncanny resemblance to their biological parents, but that, too, is not unprecedented. Like the "test tube babies" born of in vitro fertilization, cloned children need not be identifiable, much less freaks or outcasts.

Why worry so much about a few babies? Because, say opponents, even a single cloned infant puts us on the road to **genetic dystopia**, a combination of **Brave New World and Nazi Germany**. A cloned child's genetic makeup is too well known, goes the argument, and therefore transforms random reproduction into **"manufacturing"** that robs the child of his autonomy. This is where the attack broadens from nucleus transfer to human genetic engineering more generally. An anti-therapeutic cloning petition, circulated by the unlikely duo of conservative publisher William Kristol and arch-technophobe Jeremy Rifkin, concludes, "We are mindful of the **eugenics movements tragic history** of social in the first half of the 20th century, and are united in our opposition to any use of biotechnology for a commercial eugenics movement in the 21st century."

But the "eugenics" they attack has nothing to do with state-sponsored mass murder or forced sterilization. To the contrary, they are the ones who want the state to dictate the most private aspects of family life. They are the ones who want central authorities, rather than the choices of families and individuals, to determine our genetic future. They are the ones who demand that the government control the means of reproduction. They are the ones who measure the worth of human beings by the circumstances of their conception and the purity of their genetic makeup. They are the ones who say "natural" genes are the mark of true humanity.

Winners in the genetic lottery themselves, blessed with good health and unusual intelligence, they seek to deny future parents the chance to give their children an equally promising genetic start. In a despicable moral equivalency, they equate loving parents with Nazis.

Biomedicine does have the potential to alter the human experience. Indeed, it already has. Life expectancy has doubled worldwide in the past century. Childbirth is no longer a peril to mother and infant. Childhood is no longer a time for early death. The pervasive sense of mortality that down through the ages shaped art, religion, and culture has waned.

Our lives are different from our ancestors' in fundamental ways. We rarely remark on the **change**, however, because it occurred **incrementally**. That's how culture evolves and how science works. We should let the process continue.

Notice how Postrel employs logic in her effort to dilute the strength of the "fear" argument. This information resonates as "significant" and should be restated.

Postrel's point of view must be represented in your summary.

The third "fear" argument must be restated; words connoting fear are emphasized in bold font.

Notice how Postrel uses logic to refute the eugenics argument by focusing on her opponents' fear of government authorities dictating the "genetic future" of individuals. In essence, she emphasizes that the central fear of her opponents, "government control the means of reproduction," is exactly what her opponents are advocating by government banning of cloning research. Include this rhetorical turn of logic in your summary.

Postrel's ending line in this paragraph division reverberates, and should be restated to fairly represent her perspective and tone.

Some of these concrete examples highlighting scientific advancements because of steady research should be mentioned in your summary.

The repletion of this word, which appears in the first paragraph, is intentional in Postrel's narrative and essential in understanding her central idea. Your summary thesis must reflect Postrel's emphasis.

Writing the Summary

Postrel's essay has been divided into six sections, the paragraphs in each section grouped together based on the discussion of a dominant, prevailing point, idea, or theme. For example, the paragraphs in section one repeatedly restate the idea that the human cloning announcement represents rudimentary research rather than massive scientific advancement. In section five, Postrel presents, and refutes, the eugenics comparison argument. Each unit of thought in the essay needs to be concisely and fairly restated in your summary. In addition, repeated words, synonyms, and significant details from the essay that reverberate and are weighted have been highlighted and marked. Postrel begins and ends her essay with the words "incremental" and "incrementally"; the recurrence, her word choice, is intentional, for it drives home her main point that scientific breakthroughs do not happen overnight, but slowly, carefully, and in phases. These phases should be allowed to continue, she emphasizes. Once you locate this central idea, her thesis, in the essay, you must restate it precisely in content and tone.

Now work on your summary thesis. If you are still having difficulty comprehending the author's main point, wait to compose your thesis until you have summarized each division of thought and understand how each contributes to the whole. A good summary thesis should not only reveal the topic of the essay but also echo its main idea and the author's position. Suppose a student composes his thesis this way:

> Virginia Postrel says that the announcement of scientists cloning cells really is no great achievement and the government is banning it, anyway.

Is this a fair representation of the main idea of the essay? The student does restate what Postrel states. However, he does not emphasize Postrel's main point, which is that research should be allowed to continue. The student summary fails to reflect Postrel's emphasis and point of view. The summary also must include the title of the essay that the student is summarizing. Let's write a better thesis.

First, go back to the annotations. How can you minimize less important information and emphasize what Postrel emphasizes? Your sentence construction decisions are key in aiding you in this process. When you write a sentence, subordinate less important information at the beginning of your sentence, and reserve what you want to emphasize toward the sentence's end. For example, while Postrel repeatedly reminds us that the human cloning announcement was "no big deal," she emphasizes throughout the essay, and especially during her conclusion, that we continue to evolve and change, for the better, because of sustained research. Therefore, in your summary, follow her lead. State the cloning announcement in a subordinate clause, and stress her main idea in a subsequent independent clause. Your summary thesis should sound something like this:

> In "Yes, Don't Impede Medical Progress," Virginia Postrel argues that although the manufacturing of a cloned embryo in itself is no scientific breakthrough, the proposed government ban on human cloning must be rescinded since step-by-step, cumulative research holds the key for future advancements in health and culture.

Note that Postrel's position may not be yours. You may agree with the House bill prohibiting future human cloning research. When summarizing, however, your job is to fairly and truthfully restate the author's position. Nowhere should we hear your point of view. In a critique or argument essay, you may be asked to summarize an author's essay before you present your perspective. If your readers sense partiality or bias in the summary section, they may later be less accepting to listen to what you have to say in your critique or argument. Objectivity and fair representation are essential in the summary.

Now that the thesis has been written, compose a draft of the summary by following and emphasizing the main points in each bracketed unit of thought. First, begin with your thesis, and then follow with your section summaries.

Thesis

In "Yes, Don't Impede Medical Progress," Virginia Postrel argues that although the manufacturing of a cloned embryo in itself is no scientific breakthrough, the proposed government ban on human cloning must be rescinded since step-by-step, cumulative research holds the key for future advancements in health and culture.

Section 1

Researchers did produce one cloned embryo, which quickly died. Scientists believe, however, that a steady series of embryonic cell research may help them to study initial stage cell development. They hope to someday use these nascent stem cells to form specialized tissues for human treatment. Cloning research may prove less feasible for human cloning than in cell development research or in preventing deadly mutations. The purpose of continued research is to discover what we don't know.

Section 2

The word cloning itself connotes fear and hesitancy, which fuels resistance to proceed with further research. The House passed legislation forbidding not only transplantation of a nucleus for human cloning but also for any other potential uses that may be derived from the study of early cell replication. Essentially, the government has outlawed further biomedical exploration in this area. The reasons are rooted in the fear of human cloning itself.

Section 3

The first argument for the therapeutic cloning interdict is that an embryo is a human, and using its stem cells for someone else's replacement parts is unethical. Most individuals, Postrel says, do not logically or morally define one cell, or even more emerging cells, as a human being.

Section 4

Another argument is based on the fear that some unprincipled biomedical researchers, in their zeal to further their studies, would furtively insert a cloned embryo into a woman's uterus, the repercussions of which would be highly perilous for both the fetus and woman. Postrel dismisses this scenario as highly unlikely, and, instead, suggests that future sanctioned ethical research may result in healthy cloned babies for couples otherwise unable to conceive.

Section 5

Cloning opponents cite that genetic manufacturing smells like Nazi eugenics, or state dictation of desired, heritable traits or sterilization. Postrel argues that, ironically, cloning opponents themselves are the one ones advocating for state, or government, dictation of reproductive means rather than allowing individuals and families to have choices—perhaps broader choices and possibilities for individuals who want more for their children than they had—that can emerge from authorized therapeutic cloning research.

Section 6

Government-supported research has led to increased life expectancy and safer childbirth for both child and mother. Because biomedical advancement occurs gradually, we take for granted how the results have improved our lives. Biomedical research must be allowed to proceed.

The final steps in composing your summary are combining your thesis and sections summaries; matching your words with Postrel's to ensure that you are accurately restating what she says; checking that you are following Postrel's narrative sequence or order; including any other information from the original passage that resonates as significant; including effective transitions between the different thought segments; and finally, rereading and revising your sentences for flow and clarity. Note that the only sentence in your summary that may not follow the author's order is the thesis. If the author emphasizes her central point or thesis at the end of the essay, you may introduce your summary with the author's name, title of the essay, and thesis restatement, and then proceed to follow the author's sequence and emphasis. Your final summary should look something like this (additions are noted in italics):

> In "Yes, Don't Impede Medical Progress," Virginia Postrel argues that although the manufacturing of a cloned embryo in itself is no scientific breakthrough, the proposed government ban on human cloning must be rescinded since step-by-step, cumulative research holds the key for future advancements in health and culture.
>
> *While researchers used multiple eggs to ultimately clone one human embryo, which quickly died,* scientists believe that a steady series of embryonic cell research may help them to study initial stage cell development. They hope to someday use these nascent stem cells to form specialized tissues for human treatment. Cloning research, *subsequently,* may prove less feasible for human cloning than in cell development research or in preventing deadly mutations. The *impetus* of continued research, *then,* is to discover what we don't know.
>
> *For many, however,* the word cloning itself connotes fear and hesitancy, which fuels resistance to proceed with further research. The House passed legislation forbidding not only transplantation of a nucleus for human cloning, but also for any other potential uses that may be derived from the study of early cell replication. Essentially, the government has outlawed further biomedical exploration in this area. The reasons are rooted in the fear of human cloning per se.
>
> The first *fear* argument for the therapeutic cloning interdict is that an embryo is a human, and using its stem cells for someone else's replacement parts is unethical. Most individuals, Postrel says, do not logically or morally *recognize* one cell, or even more emerging cells, as a human being.
>
> *The second argument against cloning* is based on the fear that some unprincipled biomedical researchers, in their zeal to further their studies, would furtively insert a cloned embryo into a woman's uterus, the repercussions of which would be highly perilous for both the fetus and woman. Postrel dismisses this scenario as highly unlikely, and, instead, suggests that future sanctioned ethical research may result in healthy cloned babies for couples otherwise unable to conceive.

Cloning opponents *also* cite that genetic manufacturing smells like Nazi eugenics, or state dictation of desired, heritable traits or sterilization. Postrel argues that, ironically, cloning opponents themselves are the ones advocating for state, or government, dictation of reproductive means rather than allowing individuals and families to have choices—perhaps broader choices and possibilities for individuals who want more for their children than they had—that can emerge from *continued*, authorized therapeutic cloning research.

Historically, government-supported research has led to increased life expectancy and safer childbirth for both child and mother. Because biomedical advancement occurs gradually, *in careful, progressive steps*, we take for granted how the results have improved our lives. *Therefore, embryonic cell* research must be allowed to proceed.

The changes, in italics, are mostly transitions and words that improve emphasis. For example, notice how the first sentence in section two has been altered from "Researchers did produce one cloned embryo, which quickly died," to "While researchers used multiple eggs to ultimately clone one human embryo, which quickly died, scientists believe that a steady series of embryonic cell research may help them to study initial stage cell development." Less emphasis is placed on the six-cell death of the embryo. This information is deemphasized by placing it in a subordinate clause ("While researchers used multiple eggs to ultimately clone one human embryo, which quickly died"). More emphasis is placed on what Postrel emphasizes—the promise of incremental research—in the sentence's independent clause ("scientists believe that a steady series of embryonic cell research may help them to study initial stage cell development"). The independent clause comes at the ends of the sentence; it is what you are left with, and it resonates more than the subordinate clause. Transitionally and thematically, this sentence also connects better to the opening summary thesis. Notice also how the last sentence is revised. Not only is a transition included, but the more generic "biomedical research" is also changed to the more specific and emphasized "embryonic cell" research.

Now it is your turn to summarize an essay.

The Summary Assignment

Using the above strategy tips for writing a summary, summarize Erich Fromm's "Obedience as a Psychological and Moral Problem" (from *The MOON Magazine*, http://moonmagazine.org/erich-fromm-obedience-psychological-moral-problem-2014-11-30/), previously published on pages 1 to 8 of Erich Fromm's *On Disobedience and Other Essays* by Routledge Books, London, 1984).

As you read, locate Fromm's central idea and highlight the essay's major points, points you must be sure to include in your summary. You may want to make notes in the margin concerning repeated, emphasized words and ideas; demarcate distinct subdivisions of thought; and highlight significant details that should be included in the summary. A summary should be approximately one-fourth to one-third the length of the original essay, depending on essay content. Remember, in the summary, use your own words to show your understanding of the essay. Using quotation marks to replicate the exact words of the author is not a restatement, nor does it show your understanding of what you have read.

Remember to read the essay carefully, perhaps several times, before you begin to write your summary. If you are having trouble understanding the main points of the essay, you will have a difficult time clearly emphasizing these main points to your audience.

Chapter [9]

The Critique

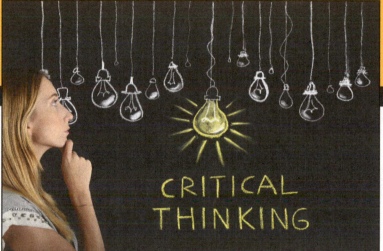

© cate_89/Shutterstock.com

Unlearning

1. Critics are basically complainers who take joy in finding fault in other people's work. Critiquing is a negative exercise that only points out flaws in writing.

2. You don't know enough about the world or about writing to critique the work of others.

3. Teachers should teach you what to think.

Relearning

1. Thinking critically involves not only fairly comprehending what an author says, but also reviewing and understanding your own prior thoughts and knowledge on a subject in order to accommodate and consider viewpoints and concepts other than your own. In this way, critiquing becomes an important way to rethink and reorganize your prior perspectives and grow both academically and personally.

2. Comprehending, analyzing, and responding to multiple points of view help you to form your own perspective. Critiquing involves judgments concerning logic that is sound versus that which is flawed.

3. The role of an instructor is to teach you *how* to think critically and for yourself, not *what* to think.

While it is true that there are individuals who get their jollies from denigrating the work of others, you should feel comfortable in an English class writing workshop to entertain multiple points of view and espouse your point of view in order to ultimately fine-comb the latter, or attempt to persuade others that your perspective has merit. *Opening your mind to other viewpoints is vital to learning and fair thinking*; you need not agree or adopt perspectives that you have analyzed as flawed. You may be surprised, however, how comprehending and entertaining other points of view can make your perspective more rational and your voice more reasonable, valued, and heard.

Ask yourself these questions: why do you think the way you think? Why are you a member of a particular political party or religious denomination? Chances are somebody else has done a lot of the thinking for you. You may simply follow the paths that your parents have prepared for you without considering alternatives. These paths may be right for you, especially if you comprehend and subscribe to the beliefs of your party or religious affiliation. Alternatively, you may unknowingly not share some or many of their principles, and yet continue to support them with your vote, attendance, or contributions. What are your views concerning gender and race, and how were they formed? Are you an individual who easily jumps on the bandwagon, who rides the tide of social messaging, or do you think things through and arrive at your *own* perspective after considering the merits and flaws of several others?

Reading and writing critically enables you to listen, consider, accept, reject, and change in order to ultimately attain your personal perspective. You will often be asked to render your opinion. Those who ask—teachers, family members, friends, job interviewers—will judge you based on your response. How often have you thought or even articulated that you do not know much about a certain subject and consequently remained silent? Worse yet, how many times have you offered 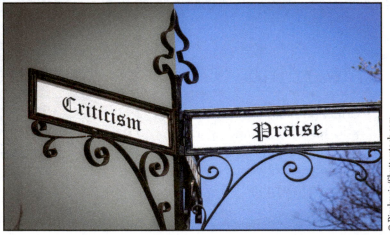 a quick opinion about a topic you know little about, ending up feeling embarrassed or unprepared for the onslaught of rebuttals? The best way to feel good about yourself and impress others is to become informed— to have already thought thoroughly about a topic after seeking multiple perspectives and by critically and fairly evaluating their merits and flaws. The last thing you should ever do is allow anyone to tell you what to think. Be skeptical of anyone, including authority figures such as teachers, who present only one point of view—theirs. The point of education is to enable you to think for yourself.

Before you can confidently form and express your point of view or write critically, you must learn how to read critically. First and foremost, critical reading necessitates reading comprehension. You must understand an author's main points, thesis, and purpose. In other words, you again must be able to summarize accurately and fairly. After your summary, you should analyze the author's presentation. Analysis includes locating the author's central idea and determining whether the author has successfully fulfilled the implied or stated purpose. Is the author convincing? Has the writer supported the main points with strong evidence? Is the evidence current, relevant, significant, and accurate? Do you see contradictions that weaken the author's main point? How do the writer's language, organization, and logic advance the author's purpose? After you analyze the presentation, you must respond to it. Evaluate whether the writer has been successful in convincing you. Quite simply, are you persuaded? Why or why not? Support your response thoroughly by using textual support to show the strengths and weaknesses you see.

In this chapter, you will be asked to focus on the analysis and evaluation of the critique. In addition, there are other components of a written critique that you must master in order for your critique to be sound and clear.

Strategy Tips: Writing the Critique

1. *Introduction and thesis*. Similar to the synthesis thesis, your introduction thesis must include the name of the author, the title of the work you are critiquing, and the author's central idea or main point. In addition, for the critique thesis, you must include your overall assessment of the author's success in fulfilling the stated or implied purpose—whether or not the writer has been successful, and the main reasons why or why not. In your introduction, you may also include general background and contextual information concerning the work, including the author's intended audience, the current relevance of the work, and pertinent biographical information about the author.

2. *Summary*. Write an objective and accurate summary, following the author's order and emphasis. Nowhere in the summary should we hear anything subjective, including your responses to what you have read. Your responses will come in subsequent sections of your critique. Refer to the strategy tips for writing the summary in Chapter 8.

3. *Exploration and analysis of the presentation*. Explore the text by continuing to use the third-person perspective to examine and assess the author's use and interpretation of information. Check the presented information for accuracy, currency, validity, fairness, and significance. Also, analyze the author's language and methods of persuasion.

Take a look at your analytical role more in detail. Suppose that a writer, in her argument against fad diets, says, "Nearly all those who lose weight, no matter what the diet program they used, gained the weight back, if not more, in one year." What questions might you have about this proclamation? The first question you may have is, "What is the source of this information?" The writer's statement may resonate more as an observation or an opinion than a fact, and facts and verifiable statistics are more accurate and valid than individual observations or opinions. Multiple, long-term studies with corroborating data from reputable sources such as medical and obesity research centers will hold more weight than a single, sweeping, uncited generalization about weight regain. Even if the writer followed her generalization with a Harvard study confirming rapidly returning weight gain after weight loss on low-carb, high-fat diets, you still should be skeptical, since this Harvard study focused on *one* diet, not all diet programs. Now suppose, later in her argument, that the writer presents a clinical study revealing that 95% of individuals who lost weight regained that weight or more in one year and claims that other studies since then have found similar results. On the surface, that 95% stat confirmed through a clinical study looks impressive—that is, until you look at the citations page and discover that the research took place in the 1950s. You should have some questions about currency and relevancy. When you research the results of the study, you find that only 100 subjects were studied and they were patients given a discharge diet without any other recorded follow-up, except for the one-year weigh-in. Are patients discharged from a hospital a representative sample or typical of the general population of current dieters? Might their outcomes be different due to the reasons for their hospital stay? Are there more and potentially better diets and dietary recommendations today? As you can see, your analysis will lead you to some reactions that you may bring up here and expound upon later in the response section of your critique.

Be aware that even though the statistics or information writers present may be accurate, their interpretation of these stats and follow-up conclusions may be faulty. For example, a writer provides ample evidence to show that the popular Mediterranean Diet may be one of the healthiest diets, but many do not lose weight until after six months, if at all, due to its higher fat content recommendations (olive oil, nuts, fatty fish) than other standard heart-healthy diets. "Therefore," the writer deduces, "if you are looking to lose weight, avoid the Mediterranean diet." In his interpretation of the accurate information he presents, the writer fails to mention the exercise regimen and serving size protocol to achieve weight loss in the Mediterranean Good Guide. Failure to provide information and oversimplification of information presented are flaws in logic that undermine evidence and persuasive efforts.

As you analyze, pay particular attention to a writer's methods of persuasion—pathos, ethos, and logos. Writers make emotional appeals (pathos), ethical appeals (ethos), and logical appeals (logos). Pathos is a method to convince or persuade through an emotional plea or response. Writers use ethical appeals (ethos) by using experts and professionals in a given field to render authority and credibility to their argument. Evidence, research, facts, figures, and sound reasoning are ways to persuade an audience logically (logos). A more thorough discussion of rhetorical strategies (pathos, ethos, and logos) follows this critique strategy list.

Finally, as you analyze the presentation, pay attention to the writer's language. How does the writer attempt to persuade you—with clearly defined words and a tone conducive to your understanding, or through words more emotionally loaded (words intended to intimidate, confuse, or manipulate) than logical?

4. *Evaluation and response to the presentation.* After you have analyzed the author's logic, language, organization, rhetorical strategies, information, and interpretation of this information, respond to the piece by demonstrating to what level you agree or disagree with the author's assessments. In this section of the critique, you provide tangible reasons for your viewpoint. Here, you may pull from what you already know about the subject, what you know from your own experiences, or what you perceive as favorable or unfavorable in the piece as far as assumptions and valid reasoning. In any case, *your* assumptions, judgments, and views are most prominent in this section. Your viewpoints should emanate predominately through the third-person perspective, although in the evaluation and response section of the critique, the first-person point of view may be appropriate.

5. *Conclusion.* Recapitulate the main points of your analysis, the author's overall success in achieving his or her purpose, and your overall reactions and judgments concerning the content of the work.

Analysis of Rhetorical Strategies in the Critique

Writers need not employ all three rhetorical devices (pathos, ethos, and logos) into each critique essay. The writer's topic and purpose should determine what devices are needed to persuade, and how.

Generally, pathos is used when a writer wants to the audience to relate, identify, or connect to the topic more emotionally or through humor. In combination with ethos (authority/credibility) and logos (logic), pathos can help the reader feel and connect with the writer's topic and concerns. For instance, it is one thing to read stats about animal abuse, abandonment, or torture, but another to read anecdotes about specific cases and pets that have been neglected or harmed. Media images augment the pathos with visuals of emaciated animals, ominous background music, and other non-textual elements. The pathos can heighten the readers' emotions and involvement in the argument. An appeal to audience emotions can be quite powerful and persuasive.

There are times, however, when an audience may feel manipulated by too much emotion—if the emotion is unearned or overwrought, or if the emotional appeals are not balanced with appeals to logic. Look carefully at a writer's word choice. Does the writer use emotionally loaded language or charged terms instead of more literal words in order to intentionally spark a quick, strong positive or negative reaction? For example, how does your reaction differ when you are told that a person "asked" versus "interrupted?" How do you react to a "crowd" of protesters verses a "mob" of protesters? Be aware of the writer's various persuasive tactics. If a reader senses a writer's blatant or biased intention to persuade, then the reader's focus will lie more on exposing the writer's method than connecting with the emotion. For example, when describing her strong relationship with her boyfriend, one student wrote that she and he often read poetry together and were often so moved that they cried "warm, moist tears." A student critic responded that the writer's language was overly sentimental, and it would have been better to "bring the relationship to life" rather than tell about the tears, since, for a reader, it is easier to feel something if you know the motivations and desires of individuals or characters. Another student said, "When are tears not moist? And what is the purpose of including 'warm,' another adjective?" Unearned heart tugging can be counterproductive in engaging and persuading your audience.

Ethical appeals can also add credibility to a writer's argument. Often, writers make their positions more credible by aligning their perspectives with those of authority figures or experts in a given field. For example, court rulings made by respected judges are often considered as authority or legal precedent for determining subsequent cases in which the issues are similar or matching. Advertisers seek the testimonials of health care professionals to recommend over-the-counter products. When you critique, however, carefully examine the credentials of the person cited as an authority. Also, don't be fooled by a person's professional title. Just because a professional is an authority in one field does not mean that person has knowledge in another area. For example, physicists and chemists hold respected degrees and their testimonies may sound impressive, yet would a physicist or chemist be the right person to promote an acne cream? The verification of an esteemed dermatologist or medical researcher, or even many of them, should hold more persuasive appeal.

Most of all, in order to persuade successfully, you must pay attention to logic. Your reasoning must be effective and your conclusion must emanate from true premises. Look closely at your premises—the propositions, statements, assumptions, assertions, evidence, and whatever else you use as the foundation or basis of your claim or conclusion. Are your propositions sound? Make sure your conclusion follows logically from true premises and valid reasoning. False conclusions can emanate not only from premises that are false but also from those that are true. Look at the following example:

Premise 1: All humans have a heart.

Premise 2: All snakes have a heart.

Conclusion: Therefore, all humans are snakes.

As you critique, point out flaws in logic, which are often unintentional lapses in reasoning. Sometimes, however, writers and speakers, in their zeal to persuade and convince, deliberately mislead in order to sell their ideas or products to a naïve audience. A good critic is capable of exposing flaws in logic and, subsequently, the intent of those who mislead.

The following are some common logical fallacies to avoid when writing and to expose when critiquing. You will also want to point out contradictions, suppressed or incomplete evidence, dubious sources, and bias. Also, remember that facts, which are verifiable, hold more argumentative weight than judgments or opinions that may not be grounded on facts.

1. An *ad hominem* reaction or argument diverts attention from a position or issue to the person maintaining that position. The focus, then, shifts from the germane topic to an irrelevant attack on the person.

   Our high school counselor means well, but what can she teach us about conflict resolution strategies? She's divorced.

2. Writers often support their claims with evidence from reputable authorities in a given field. Sometimes, however, writers **appeal to false authorities** and accept their claims merely because they admire them and without verifying the veracity of their statements or the credentials of the "experts."

   Sixteen hour intermittent fasting has proven to be one of the best diets ever as manifested by the testimonies of many Hollywood celebrities who have remained fit for years.

3. An **appeal to pity** argument attempts to persuade by appealing to, and concentrating on, emotional, irrelevant feelings of sympathy rather than evidence and the real issue present.

   His resume shows a lack of education and experience for this job, but we should hire him because his wife is also unemployed.

4. When a writer or speaker suggests that you should do or believe something simply because many or most people do, the entreaty used

© WAYHOME studio/Shutterstock.com

is the **bandwagon fallacy**. Advertisers commonly promote their products this way to make consumers believe that if they do not join the crowd, then they will be lacking or falling behind in some way. Politicians also use the bandwagon fallacy to suggest constituents will be missing out if they do not jump on the rising tide and follow the trend.

A recent poll revealed that 59% of registered voters will vote for Henry Smith for city council. Won't you join them?

5. **Begging the question**, or circular reasoning, is a logically flawed form of reasoning that lacks evidence for the stated conclusion. Instead of evidence, the writer posits the premises as truth and repeats the same "truth" in the conclusion rather than supports the conclusion. In essence, what is stated in premise is restated in the conclusion.

Men are not suited for child-rearing because it is not their nature to bring up children.

6. **Either/or reasoning** suggests that only two options exist and neglects to recognize alternatives. Often, the two options stated are extremes; the writer fails to acknowledge other possibilities or choices in order to steer the audience to the "right side."

I know this house is costly, but either we buy it now or we may end up living in a shack for the rest of our lives.

7. **Equivocation** is the intentional or unconscious use of vague, ambiguous, or confusing wording to circumvent the truth or to evade a definitive response. Often, writers equivocate or vacillate by using different meanings of the same word.

Government leaders should not force the use of face masks to prevent the spread of disease because that masks a bigger problem.

© i_photos/Shutterstock.com

8. An analogy is a comparison drawn usually for the purpose of clarifying or explaining. A **false analogy** is the false assumption that because two things are alike in one way, they are alike in other ways.

Grace and Hannah are both elementary school teachers. They both then must want to have a lot of children of their own someday.

9. Assuming that something resulted after another event without showing a causal relationship between the two is a fallacy of **false cause**.

Ever since the borough resurfaced our streets, crime rates have dropped significantly.

10. *Assumptions based on one person's experience, opinion, study, or small sample sizes often are not representative or applicable to the wider population.* **Generalizations** are broad, sweeping, often hasty conclusions and statements based on too little evidence. All-inclusive words such as all, always, anyone, everyone, never, and none often lead to assumptions lacking representative and ample evidence. Generalizations can lead to stereotypes.

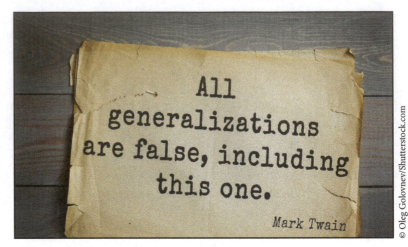

All generalizations are false, including this one.

Mark Twain

Men are never as sensitive and caring as women.

Everyone loves to tan at the beach.

Learning a new language is always problematic.

11. A *non sequitur* is a conclusion, statement, or inference that does not follow logically from a premise. *Non sequiturs* omit a logical connection between two statements.

She bought a new cutlery set and put her dogs up for adoption.

12. As the name suggests, **oversimplification** is the fallacy of rendering a seemingly simplistic, easy explanation or solution by ignoring, concealing, or failing to detect more complex factors involved with an issue or problem.

The banning of spray deodorants will solve our global warming issue.

13. A **red herring** is a logical fallacy that an arguer uses to distract or mislead in order to divert an audience's attention from the real, original problem, issue, or person of interest.

My client did admit shooting the plaintiff, but if you put him in jail, who will take care of his two sickly, elderly parents?

14. A **slippery slope** argument warns that the occurrence or allowance of one action will open the gates to a chain of unfortunate or harmful consequences. Often, these proposed ensuing consequences are ridiculous and purely hypothetical.

If the government bans cigarette smoking, the next prohibition will be alcohol, soda, cream puffs, and anything else, that in extreme excess, can be bad for you.

15. A card dealer who arranges the deck in a way to ensure that the cards he deals himself will achieve the result he wants is said to stack the deck. In literature, **stacking the deck** is a type of propaganda in which the writer or speaker reveals only certain cards—only evidence that supports his point of view. A writer who flatly rejects, ignores, or omits evidence supporting the counterargument and shows only his evidence is guilty of stacking the deck. For example, a car advertisement that cites its lowest price per comparable model but fails to reveal that it has the lowest vehicle reliability and safety ratings stacks the deck.

16. An arguer who misrepresents the original argument and distorts it because the weaker, extreme substitute argument is easier to defeat has committed the **straw man** fallacy. The straw man strategy is a strategy of avoidance—that is, a way to circumvent the merits of the opposing viewpoint.

    So when you advocate for strengthening the military you ignore the more pressing issues of allocation of funds for the homeless and for our deteriorating environment.

Remember, when you critique, also point out what *is* valuable in a writer's argument; what is weighted and needs be expanded upon; and logic, pathos, and ethos that resound as convincing. Has the writer included varied, credible sources and stats that reinforce the main point of the argument? Does the writer stay focused in supporting the thesis? How does the argument build? Does the writer include, and successfully quell, opposing points of view? What advice do you have for revision or for further discussion?

The Critique Assignment

Here are some argument essays written by first-year college students. Using the guidelines above for writing the critique, analyze and respond to the following student essays.

Legal Drinking Age

Rory Dami

Drinking in our nation it is frowned upon unless you are twenty-one, but should it be? I believe it should not. Once we get to our junior and senior year of high school and into college is when most of us are really faced with this choice. Most of us have been invited to a huge party where there is going to be alcohol. Most people will tell kids to just say no to drinking and leave but in all reality, it is not that easy to say no. All of your friends are around you and trying to hand you a drink and saying come on nothing is going to happen. They are all right if you know how to handle yourself and be responsible with drinking. I believe the drinking age should be lowered because when you turn eighteen you are an adult in the eyes of the law, teens will still drink even though it is illegal, it could stop the practice of unsafe underage drinking, and it could lower the number of fatal drunk driving accidents and fatalities.

In my opinion I believe that the legal drinking age in the United States should be lowered to eighteen. Whenever you turn eighteen, you are looked at as a legal adult in the eyes of the law and court ("Should the

Drinking"). If I am going to be tried as an adult in a criminal act then I should be treated as a complete adult in the eyes of the law. There are many things that becoming eighteen affect like using tobacco, playing the lottery, getting married, joining the military, and even serving as a jury member. If when I turn eighteen I can do all these things, why am I not allowed to have a beer at the end of a long, stressful day? Some of the things that I listed are way more important than drinking. Going overseas to fight in a war is much more serious than simply drinking. They say only adults should drink alcohol, but if I am held to these other standards as an adult, then why am I not one when it comes to the consumption of alcohol?

Think of this number, 7.3 million. That is the number of people between the age of 12 and 20 that consumed alcohol in 2017 ("Underage Drinking Statistics"). This number proves that even though the drinking age is 21 people are still going to drink. Whenever most students go to college they think about parties and drinking and having a good time. They know that they are not allowed to drink under the age of 21 but do you think that stops them? Most people know what happens at frats and fraternities at the big schools and even some of the small ones around the country. In one survey 63% of college students reported to drinking underage ("Underage Drinking Statistics"). Why fight what you know is happening regardless of the law?

If you lower the legal drinking age and young adults 18 and up are allowed to drink then it will stop the practice of unsafe underage drinking for the most part ("Should the Drinking"). If a kid in college wants to drink and he is able to go to a bar and drink where he will be around other people in the bar he is more likely to act appropriately when drinking and not go overboard. If he is forced to secretly drink at a party that he has to keep quiet, he is more likely to drive and get home so nothing is suspicious and no one thinks that he was drinking. If he is allowed to drink he can call an Uber or a friend to pick him up and just return to get his car the next day to ensure their safety and no one will question and soon find out he was underage drinking.

Going global with the statistics, countries with a legal drinking age of 18 have a lower rate of drunk driving traffic accidents and fatalities ("Should the Drinking"). If we want to lower how many people are injured and killed because of drinking and driving then this is proof alone to support that. Most Americans think that we always have to be the leader, but it is not always a bad thing to be a follower once in a while to better yourself a little bit. It has been 24 years since the United States raised the legal drinking age and I believe it is time that we lower it once again back to 18 years old.

Even though I believe it should be lowered I do understand that there are several downsides to lowering the drinking age. When we are 18 some of us are still not yet completely developed ("Should the Drinking"). Consuming alcohol has been proven to mess with the development of brain growth, function, and many other developmental factors. If we mess with the development of our body, it may not affect us now, but it possibly could in the future. It is proven that when brain development is altered that suicide, depression, and violence rates go up on average. A solution to this though is keeping up with doctor visits to make sure and monitor that you are healthy with the habits you are partaking in. Even without drinking alcohol it is healthy and recommended to make doctor checkups more regularly.

If the drinking age was lowered to 18 it could give easier access to kids under 18 to consume alcohol ("Should the Drinking"). If you think about it most seniors in high school are 18 or even 19 which would make them old enough to purchase and consume alcohol. This would make it a lot easier for younger kids to get their hands on it and possibly lead to them getting caught with it and punished by the law. This also poses the threat of alcohol being brought to school and causing issues there as well. High school principals and faculty should not have to deal with students coming to school intoxicated or becoming intoxicated during the school day. A solution to this like my old high school did was not allowing any open bottles in the school throughout the day. They should only allow bottles that were bought from the school during lunch time to be out during lunch periods only.

Another major reason that the drinking age should not be lowered is because a study showed that the younger a person began to consume alcohol the more likely they were to begin to use illicit drugs ("Should the Drinking"). We surely do not want our young adults to start doing illegal and harmful drugs that will ruin their future. This could also lead to more crime that would spread across the nation and cause a global conflict that would ultimately hard to contain. A very easy solution to this is just have the police force monitor the streets more often to see if they recognize any suspicious behavior. When it comes to schools and drugs, have the local police force come up randomly throughout the year with the K-9 unit to sniff the hallways to track down any drugs students may be possessing.

The statistics line up for and against the lowering of the legal drinking age in this country. Although the cons are pretty severe I still believe that lowering the drinking age would not affect the country that greatly. There are several solutions to the cons that people could look into to help stop all the negative things that go along with lowering the legal drinking age. If young adults can prove that they can handle it responsibly, then I believe they should lower the drinking age. When you become 18 you are looked as an adult and are expected to act like one, and in return we expect to be treated like one.

Works Cited

"Should the Drinking Age Be Lowered from 21 to a Younger Age?" *ProCon.org*, 11 September 2017, drinkingage.procon.org/

"Underage Drinking Statistics." *Foundation for Advancing Alcoholic Responsibility*, www.responsibility.org/get-the-facts/research/statistics/underage-drinking-statistics/

Chuck E. Cheese: More Like Chuck E. Sleaze

Michael Connelly

Almost every child in America has seen or attended a Chuck E. Cheese. These establishments are "family fun centers" that hold arcade games and activities, at a price, for the opportunity to win tickets. The tickets obtained can be cashed in for prizes such as candy, stuffed animals, and toys. These centers also sell food and beverages, as well as act as a means for holding parties for young children. At a first glance this establishment showcases all good qualities, but after further evaluation, some of the games that children play employ an underlying method of gambling. Chuck E. Cheese does hold positive

© Susan Montgomery/Shutterstock.com

aspirations in the aspect that they wish to create an outlet for children to have fun with games and activities. Not all the games at Chuck E. Cheese elicit such hidden implications, but involving children in such schemes allows kids to be exposed to gambling at a young age and should not be allowed.

When discussing the possible notion that gambling is prevalent in such establishments, the word gambling must be defined. The Merriam-Webster definition for gambling is "to play a game for money or property" ("Gambling"). In the case of arcade games at Chuck E. Cheese, children are required to pay money for access to these games. In consequence, children's parents most often, or the children themselves, pay money to play a game for tickets. These tickets, in the context of the definition, are considered property. Property is defined as "something owned or possessed," and the acquisition of tickets at Chuck E. Cheese fulfills the definition ("Property"). Also, in the definition of gambling, the action of "bet[ting] on an uncertain outcome" is very prevalent in a number of games that are in a Chuck E. Cheese ("Gambling"). Customers are spending money and in return they are not guaranteed the quantity of their outcome beforehand and that is therefore "uncertain." Therefore, at Chuck E. Cheese, children are lured to gambling-like activities that are showcased and have been encouraged to take part in by children for generations.

As the implication of gambling does not reside in all games at Chuck E. Cheese, there are still some that fulfill the definition of gambling. There are some games at Chuck E. Cheese that require skill such as car racing, Tetris, Whac-A-Mole, and others, but some of the games within Chuck E. Cheese are based on pure luck. Such games are very similar to slot machines in which both facilities are played by pulling a lever or handle, and after that the machine spins and outputs its result, regardless of player skill or experience. According to the U.S. legal definition, gambling is "playing any game of chance, for money or other thing of value ("Gambling Law"). Using this definition, alongside the Merriam-Webster definition, some of the games within Chuck E. Cheese fulfill the designation of gambling. At these establishments, children consistently play games of chance, such as the "spin the wheel" or "roulette" games that are undeniably based upon luck and chance. The majority of children who would play such games are very young and have not fully developed their brain yet, and therefore often they act more impulsively, take more risks, and do not fully consider the consequences of their actions ("The Dangers"). Consequently, this causes children to feel more inclined to play games when they have lost repeatedly, hoping to perform better on their next try, although the game they are playing is purely based on luck. This creates a problem for children and their parents since children playing such games may not fully comprehend that they are losing at a game of chance.

The average Chuck E. Cheese advocate would battle such claims with the notion that if Chuck E. Cheese allowed children to gamble, how could it be legal? There is no way that a company as large as Chuck E. Cheese would permit such illegal activity unnoticed. Not to mention that if such game activities for children are "gambling," then the momentum that society can build with exposing such companies would have already built, and the company would have already been shut down and dire consequences would have been enacted. The youngest age that someone can gamble in the United States is 18, so in what way could an establishment such as Chuck E. Cheese, a "family establishment," allow for such illegal interactions?

The machines in the establishment escape the legal claims of being considered gambling by giving the customer at least something for their payment. True gambling includes the chance of losing all property that is risked upon being gambled. Regardless of the machine in Chuck E. Cheese, the customer is guaranteed at least one ticket, but the possibility of receiving more tickets is based entirely on chance, or based upon talent for the games that require skill. The method of receiving a minimum ticket amount distinguishes the games as being "true" schemes of gambling, but how the tickets are used to turn-in for prizes showcases that the one ticket minimum is essentially the equivalent of losing money and fulfilling the requirement of gambling. Taking the minimum ticket reward amount into consideration, some of the prizes that can be purchased by redeeming tickets cost upwards to 5,000 tickets! These rewards that are sold for ridiculous prices cost only a couple dozen dollars to purchase in a store or online. Hypothetically, if each spin from a machine of chance cost 50 cents and the customer received only one ticket per spin, which is possible, it would cost them 2,500 dollars for a toy or stuffed animal that retails for only 40 or 50 dollars.

Children who play games at Chuck E. Cheese see the prizes that they can purchase with tickets and become motivated to play games to earn enough tickets for the biggest prize. This "drive," especially in younger kids, encourages the child to play more games to earn enough tickets to get their favorite stuffed animal or best toy. Children are more susceptible to these schemes in the notion that they act more impulsively and fail to think situations through fully before taking into consideration the consequences of their own actions. Although some will argue these interactions are not technically gambling, the idea and motive to get customers to pay money to continuously partake in a game of chance are the same motives present in casinos and poker tables. These interactions can be particularly harmful, since "studies have shown that children who are introduced to and begin gambling by age 12 are four times more likely to become problem gamblers ("The Dangers").

Another claim that can be made by Chuck E. Cheese supporters to protect the establishment is that customers pay for an experience, and the tickets and prizes are just an added bonus. Families pay for their children to play games and the idea of obtained tickets for prizes is just an added commodity. People shouldn't complain if they don't earn enough tickets for prizes since they technically don't even deserve the tickets for the prizes in the first place and Chuck E. Cheese could have just opted to be an arcade with no prizes involved, but they chose to add them.

This argument is partially true, but this claim does not apply to all games at Chuck E. Cheese. The games that the claim does apply to are games such as ski-ball, basketball, air hockey, racing games, etc. that require skill and are considered fun. The games that this does not apply to more importantly are the exact games that subtly employ methods of disguised gambling. These games are the "roulette' and "spin the wheel" games that are predominantly luck or chance. These are the games that are exposing children to subtle forms of gambling. The idea that a customer, *a child*, would pay to play these games and expect to receive nothing in return as the counterargument claims is absurd.

Although not all the games and machines within Chuck E. Cheese elicit implications of underlying gambling, there are still some machines that are placed within such establishments for that exact purpose. The reasoning for creating such "games" is to draw children into playing them repeatedly due to the drive for tickets for a prize that is practically unobtainable. This drive creates a motivation for young children that is similar to casino, slot machine gambling. The employment of such devices should not be enacted as it exposes young kids to such activities reserved for an older audience, and rightfully so, as it has the opportunity to make children four times more likely to become problem gamblers. Chuck E. Cheese should remove such machines and stick to providing a genuine and fun experience to the children of this generation rather than selling disguised forms of gambling to young kids.

Works Cited

"Gambling." *Merriam-Webster.com Dictionary*, Merriam-Webster, www.merriam-webster.com/dictionary/gambling

"Gambling Law and Legal Definition." Fraud Law and Legal Definition, definitions.uslegal.com/g/gambling/

"Property." *Merriam-Webster.com Dictionary*, Merriam-Webster, www.merriam-webster.com/dictionary/property

"The Dangers of Youth Gambling Addiction." Knowtheodds.org, knowtheodds.org/wp-content/uploads/2013/05/NYCPG_ebook_YouthGambling_052114.pdf.

Perfect Parents: A Plea for Homosexuals and Adoption Rights

Leah Barrett

Imagine a young man growing up in America. He attends school, finds a job, experiences new people and events, learning and realizing his character, his goals, his desires, his beliefs. Imagine others disagreeing with him over a certain decision, opinion, preference. Imagine him being judged, criticized, tormented, not just by them but by perhaps even himself. Imagine him struggling to feel and be accepted, perhaps even attempting to take his life. Imagine him persevering and finding someone he believes to be the love of his life; someone he wants to share the rest of his days with. This could be someone who has dealt with and may still deal with his same struggles, but this time they will walk together. They form a union, and after a while desire for something greater, in fact the *greatest* something; something to love and nurture, something that will outlive them and carry on their memories and name, something to complete the picture: a child. This, however, can be denied to them in some cases. Why? *This couple is of the same sex.*

Homosexuality has been present since the beginning of humanity, yet it has gotten much attention and progression in the previous century and these last few decades. Homosexual marriage was not legalized in America until 2004, when it was allowed in Massachusetts. It was not legalized in all fifty states until 2015, after the victory of *Obergefell v. Hodges* in which the US Supreme Court determined that same-sex marriage is constitutional ("What to Know"). With this groundbreaking development, adoption for homosexual couples was immediately requested—and questioned. Children needing loving homes have been denied from those seeking to expand their family, because of the objections that children should be raised in heterosexual households, that they will be subjected to the stigmas associated with the parents, and that it goes against the religious beliefs of certain agencies.

Adoption rights for homosexual couples must be protected, as it is a constitutional right, children must leave the adoption/foster care system, and it is an absolute natural right and privilege for anyone to have a family.

After decades of cases and controversy, there are currently no federal laws whatsoever prohibiting homosexuality and the ability for anyone to become guardians. In perusing the Constitution, one can see this. A promise from Amendment I establishes the fact that the United States of American was not, is not, and never will be a theocracy, and therefore the rights of homosexuals cannot be denied due to religious reasons: "Congress shall make no law respecting an establishment of religion, or prohibiting the free exercise thereof." Article I of Amendment XIV may be applied to protect these rights, *as homosexuals are still American citizens*: "All persons born or naturalized in the United States, and subject to the jurisdiction thereof, are citizens of the United States and of the State wherein they reside. No State shall make or enforce any law which shall abridge the privileges or immunities of citizens of the United States; nor shall any State deprive any person of life, liberty, or property, without due process of law; nor deny to any person within its jurisdiction the equal protection of the laws." The legalization of these marriages makes the affirmation that they are no less legitimate or less recognized than a heterosexual marriage (Baltzell).

More than 23,000 children age out of the foster care and adoption system every year. 20% become instantly homeless, 70% of girls become pregnant before they are 21, 60% of boys become incarcerated, and 25% do not pass high school. They can become prostitutes and be trafficked ("51 Useful"). They may also development resentment, inferiority complex, and depression ("Psychological Effects"). Children in single-parent households can experience similar detrimental impacts. Michael Hullett, who works with Therapeutic Interventions, Inc., a foster care and adoption agency in Tennessee, solemnly stated: "To deny people the opportunity to help those kids is a disgrace" ("US: LGBT Parents") Moreover, one of the reasons the Constitution was established was to promote the general welfare. There is a clear obligation to help as many kids as possible. Ushering them into the loving, eager arms of awaiting homosexual couples is the best possible way and is for the greater good given these troubling statistics.

The first definition of family is "the basic unit in society traditionally consisting of two parents rearing their children *also*: any of various social units differing from but regarded as equivalent to the traditional family" ("Family"). Children have the amazing ability to make people happy. They give one greater purpose and inspire learning. They make families complete. Having and raising children is a command, the highest and most natural calling of human beings. Homosexuals *are* human beings *and* citizens of the US. To deny these personal obligations to someone perfectly capable of nurturing would be wrong and heartbreaking not just for those seeking to adopt, but also for the child seeking a family of their own, while waiting in the system and being bounced around in different homes. Both the Preamble of the Constitution and Amendment XIV can be used to protect the wishes of homosexual couples to adopt. The Declaration of Independence may also be cited: "We hold these truths to be self-evident, that all men are created equal, that they are endowed by their Creator with certain unalienable Rights, that among these are Life, Liberty and the pursuit of Happiness.--That to secure these rights, Governments are instituted among Men, deriving their just powers from the consent of the governed--"

One opposing argument against homosexual adoption is that every child requires a father and a mother to provide balance. This becomes even more critical if an adopted child is coming from a single-parent home. A father is there to be the main leader, provider, protector, the one issuing discipline. He is there to teach his son how to be strong and self-reliant, how to handle obstacles, how to act and communicate with other men, how to take care of his body when it changes. He is there to protect his daughter from men who may harm her, to hold her when she cries, to walk her down the aisle, to rejoice with her when she has children of her own. A mother is there to be attentive and care for her children's needs, to mediate, to assist, to soothe, to learn who her children are, what they want, and what their futures may look like. She is there to teach her daughter how to accept her outer and inner beauty, how to behave in public and in the presence of company, what qualities she should look for in a husband, how to recover from misfortunes, how to take care of her body when it changes. She is there to guide her son in making good choices, how to be patient, how to be a gentleman, what qualities to look for in a wife. These contrasts cannot be present in a household with two fathers or two mothers. Katy Faust, who was actually raised by two mothers, agreed and advocated that a second mother is no replacement for a father: "Whether you're heterosexual or homosexual, children have rights. It needs to be on adults to conform to the rights of children, rather than children fitting into an adult's lifestyle" ("Child").

A second opposing argument is that children adopted by homosexuals will suffer judgement and scrutiny by their peers and others who disapprove of their parents and their choices. Homosexuals have long been in the minority, in the shadows and sewers of society. They have been considered sinful, godless, mentally defective, confused, weak, rebellious, and even predatory. No one, no *parent*, wants to see a child affiliated with those titles. A child may already have a hard time being accepted and coming to terms with their adoptive background, but to also deal with this? Having a child be subjected to such controversy could be considered a form of abuse. A study conducted in 2008 for US children K-12 revealed that 40% of those being raised in a same-sex household reported harassment, and 23% did not feel safe in school due to their family orientation. Along with this comes verbal abuse and subtle or non-subtle moments of being ignored and despised (Vitelli).

Perhaps the most powerful opposition to homosexual adoption are the protests of certain religion-based agencies. On February 25 of this year, the US Supreme Court agreed to hear an appeal submitted by Catholic Social Services, who claims they may lose their government contract as a result of not certifying homosexual couples as possible foster parents (Vogue). This poses a problem as other agencies across the country have closed, and more and more children are coming into the system. The First Amendment can be applied here in *their* defense as well. They do not wish to give impressionable children to those whose lifestyle they do not agree with and believe is sinful. They believe giving these children away to these individuals could be considered a sin in itself. They may also fear that they will absorb and support the ideals of their adoptive parents and even sinning by become homosexuals themselves. Multiple verses in the Holy Bible are used to condemn homosexuality, which many Christians have stood by and will continue to do so in various degrees and ways. Starting in the book of Genesis on 2:20-22, a second human is created by God: "But for Adam no suitable helper was found. So the Lord God caused the man to fall into a deep sleep; and while he was sleeping, He took one of the man's ribs and then closed up the place with flesh. Then the Lord God made a woman from the rib he had taken out of the man, and He brought her to the man." God appears to be setting a precedent—it is a man and woman that are paired together and have sexual relations later to experience pleasure and to spread their kind across the earth, as they were commanded to do. In the book of Leviticus, in 18:22 and 20:13, the Israelites are commanded *twice*, very clearly, that a man should never have sexual relations with another man. Doing this was worthy of death. The Bible's New Testament confirms that homosexuality is still wrong in the eyes of God with 1 Corinthians 6:9-10: "Or do you not know that wrongdoers will not inherit the kingdom of God? Do not be deceived: neither the sexually immoral nor idolaters nor men who have sex with men nor thieves nor the greedy nor drunkards nor slanderers nor swindlers will inherit the kingdom of God" (Allberry).

No, many do not agree with homosexuality and the rights asked for and may never will. Homosexuality will always remain a debated topic in society, and that can and should be accepted. The main issue here, however, is the adopted children. Is it *always* best to have one mother and one father? Heterosexual parents may conflict with each other and cause tension in the household, and roughly half of marriages today result in divorce. The ideal tasks of mothers and fathers have also been called extremely sexist and outdated. Furthermore, homosexual couple cannot have children by accident—they intend to have and support any and all of them. It takes months, years of planning and processing for them to finally obtain the children they've been waiting for and start their family.

Children and even adults have always been in danger of being bullied and feeling uncomfortable, as a result of multiple factors. However, as same-sex parents experienced struggle in their lifetime, they will be more empathetic and impress their resilience onto their children. It is now 2020: people have become more aware the homosexual community, and as it has become more open throughout the world, it has seemed more "normal," resulting in more tolerance and acceptance.

As stated before, the United States of America was established as a democracy, not a theocracy. Homosexual couples should not be forced to pay taxes and funding towards organizations that discriminate against them. However, *both* sides are defended by Amendment I.

In conclusion, the adoption rights of homosexuals are a critical issue in the U.S. All citizens and human beings have rights, natural and constitutional, and children must be put into stable homes where they will be secure and successful.

Works Cited

Allberry, Sam. "What Does the Bible Say about Homosexuality?" *Living Out*, www.livingout.org/the-bible-and-ssa

Baltzell, George W. "Constitution of the United States—We the People." *Constitution for the United States—We the People*, constitutionus.com/.

"Child of lesbian parents opposes gay marriage" (2015) | ABC News (Australia), www.youtube.com/watch?v=V73Y1HsDKWs

"Family." *Merriam-Webster*, Merriam-Webster, www.merriam-webster.com/dictionary/family

"51 Useful Aging Out of Foster Care Statistics: Social Race Media." *National Foster Youth Institute*, 26 May 2017, www.nfyi.org/51-useful-aging-out-of-foster-care-statistics-social-race-media/

"The Psychological Effects of Living with a Single Parent." *Secureteen.com*, 30 August 2016, www.secureteen.com/single-dad/negative-psychological-effects-of-a-single-parent-family-on-children/

"US: LGBT Parents Face Adoption Discrimination" Human Rights Watch, www.youtube.com/watch?v=d6E-b9LsSTS8

Vitelli, Romeo. "Gay Parents and the Fight for Acceptance." *Psychology Today*, Sussex Publishers, 21 December 2016, https://www.psychologytoday.com/us/blog/media-spotlight/201612/gay-parents-and-the-fight-acceptance

Vogue, Ariane de. "Supreme Court Takes up Religious Liberty Dispute on Foster Care and Same-Sex Marriage." *CNN*, Cable News Network, 24 February 2020, www.cnn.com/2020/02/24/politics/supreme-court-same-sex-foster-care-agency/index.html

"What to Know About the History of Same-Sex Adoption." *Considering Adoption*, consideringadoption.com/adopting/can-same-sex-couples-adopt/history-of-same-sex-adoption

In-Class Activities

1. *Thesis wars*

   Your instructor will select an essay or article from this book, or from a journal, newspaper, or magazine, and place you in a group of three or four. Each group will compose a critique thesis for the chosen piece. One member from each group will write the group's critique thesis on the board, and the class as a whole will judge which thesis is best, and why.

2. *Point-Counterpoint*

   Look again at the three student essays in this chapter, and, for each, consider the counterclaims. Compose several possible points supporting the opposing point of view. After you have considered both sides of the argument, decide which side you believe has the most weighted argument, and represent that team in a class debate concerning the topic.

ADDITIONAL ASSIGNMENTS

1. Critique an advertisement either from a magazine or a television commercial. Print the ad or record the commercial and give a five-minute presentation highlighting the strengths and weaknesses of the ad. What is the intended demographic for the ad? Are the emotional, ethical, and/or logical appeals successful in reaching and persuading this target audience? What, specifically, are these appeals? Is the information presented valid, accurate, and significant? What is the claim, and is there sufficient evidence to back the claim? What is that evidence? What details or visuals enhance or distract from this claim? Approach this assignment not only as a critic, but also as a consumer.

2. Critique a newspaper editorial or an essay opinion blog. Be sure to include the opinion piece with your critique.

3. Find a recently published short story (fiction) in a literary journal. After you have finished reading the story, ask yourself if you found the story engaging and worth your time. Examine the success of the author's use of characterization, narrative sequence, rising tension, plot, imagery, use of dialogue, beginning, ending, and anything else that contributed to, or took away from, your level of engagement.

4. Examine the brand logos of ten corporations and list them from least to most effective in creatively identifying the company, brand, or product. Be specific in your analysis concerning the details of each logo.

5. Provide a written critique of a syllabus from one of your current instructors.

6. Write a critique of Virginia Postrel's "Yes, Don't Impede Medical Progress" (see Chapter 8).

Chapter [10]

Descriptive Writing

© aleriy Boyarskiy/Shutterstock.com

Unlearning

1. Abstract words such as "courageous," "talented," "big," "beautiful," and "friendship" are excellent words to use to describe and appeal to your audience's senses.

2. Clichés are useful in descriptive writing since their meanings are easily and quickly understood by many and, thus, are a succinct way to convey certain images or ideas.

3. Descriptive writing is "flowery" writing that often smothers and interferes with a writer's true purpose or meaning.

Relearning

1. Abstract words stand for ideas, qualities, notions, ideals, concepts, and feelings that are intangible and cannot be easily felt or experienced through your senses. Also, abstract language is more general language and can be confusing or unclear to the reader since it can mean different things to different people. Concrete language is clear language that more directly appeals to the senses. Unlike abstract words, we can see, hear, smell, taste, touch—we can experience—concrete words.

2. Trite words, familiar plots, and stereotyped characters fail to engage most readers. While clichés can be quick ways to convey ideas or images, your audience will be bored reading what they have read and seen many times before.

3. Concrete language can convey more intellectually and emotionally in fewer words than general language that fails to engage or appeal to the senses of the audience.

© Yury Zap/Shutterstock.com

Elaborating on an example used in Chapter 6 concerning the differences between showing and telling, read the first few lines of an essay written by a student describing what is meaningful to her:

Sherry is my best friend. We do everything together. She is loyal and courageous. She always has my back. I know she will always be there for me when I need her.

Ask yourself this question: Are you interested? There are many reasons you may not be engaged at this point. First of all, what distinguishes this friendship from other friendships? What stands out here that sustains your interest? How many clichés do you see in these first five sentences? What is the narrator like? What is Sherry like? What sensory details draw you into the narrative? What does the writer show instead of tell? What are your expectations at the onset—that you will be drawn into a narrative that makes you feel as if you are there, observing and feeling what the student observed and felt *at that moment in time*, or that you will hear a common, familiar, general account that you have heard before?

Next, address the clichés. You may have the following questions at the onset. What does "best friend" mean? How do the dynamics of this friendship differ from those of other "best" friendships? Showing, at the onset, will be better than simply telling so that we can witness the subtleties of the friendship. Second, you may ask the writer this: you "do everything together"? Look at how vague the word "everything" is. May some readers think that it may be kind of creepy that you do "everything together"? And why does Sherry "always" need to "have your back"? What might that suggest about you? *You, the writer*, may know that Sherry "will always be there for [you] when [you] need her," but does the audience know enough about you or Sherry to feel that? The clichés, rather than distinguishing characters and details, take over at the beginning of this essay, and many readers may say that they know very little, or nothing, at this point. Quite frankly, many simply will not care to read anything more.

Now look at the abstract words used in these opening lines. What does loyal mean to you? Does loyalty always have a positive connotation? Do you admire a spouse's loyalty to a partner who is inattentive, insulting, or unfaithful? Are there varying degrees of loyalty, ranging from a dog's loyalty to its owner, a congregant's loyalty to his church, a citizen's loyalty to her country, or a slave's loyalty to his master? While "loyalty," in general, may suggest something positive, in the context of the student's opening, you don't know nearly enough about the characters yet to make a judgement. You are asked to "take the author's word for it" rather than make your own conclusions based on what you see and hear. If you are not invited to form own judgements and ideas by using your senses, but instead are simply rendered general, vague information, you will not be engaged should the narrative proceed the way it began. Readers want to be engaged, involved, and interpret for themselves.

Again, abstract words can mean different things to different people. Loyalty to a church or state that has proven, altruistic outreach is one thing, but loyalty to a church or state that misappropriates funds or abuses its members is another. Should you be more loyal to people and organizations than to the principles and values that you hold?

The student writer also tells us Sherry is "courageous." How? She may not be afraid of insects. Is that your definition of courageous? Instead of telling, show us how Sherry is courageous. Allow your audience to witness her courage without your telling us. Let your readers form their own impression by using their senses. Sherry's courage may be physical, emotional, moral, intellectual, or social. The reader simply won't know or feel it at this point. Again, abstract words lend themselves to various and vague interpretations. Be specific. Be concrete. Show instead of tell.

Do you know of parents who label their children "talented"? Do you always agree with their assessment when you witness the children's performances or work? At least you had the chance to observe—to see or hear or taste or smell or touch. You had the opportunity to draw your own conclusions based on your senses and also your sense of reason. When someone merely writes that someone else is talented, the abstraction falls flat, and you are not invited to observe. You are not invited into the narrative. You, the audience, are not truly considered.

Now look at how the student revised her opening sentences after listening to peer criticism.

> *I stretched to look at Sherry's answers, but as soon as she noticed she put her hand over the exam. Each fingernail was a different color, and she moved her fingers rhythmically as if the exam were a keyboard. Was she ever still?*

> *She finished first, waiting for me outside the biology lab, running in place. "Pizza," she said. "We deserve pizza. At least I do."*

> *"What was that?" I said.*

> *She took my hand and led me down the hall. I could smell rising dough and cheesy sauce, but that was all in my mind. We were still in the lab hall.*

> *"You could have helped me," I said.*

> *"I did," she said, facing me directly, her eyes unapologetic. "Study next time. You're better than that."*

Concrete descriptive language need not be flowery language. In fact, often it is quite the opposite. It is to the point, vivid, exact, and allows readers to make their own judgments and evoke their own feelings about characters, motives, relationships, and events. In the revised opening, what do you know about the characters that you didn't know in the original version? Moreover, what judgments are you making about the characters and their relationship that you could not make in the original passage? How and why are you more involved? What words appeal to your senses? How does showing allow you to participate in the narrative and entice you to continue to read and find out what happens next?

Follow the criteria for successful descriptive writing.

Strategy Tips: Descriptive Writing

1. *Establish your central idea, theme, and purpose.* What distinguishes your subject for your audience? How is this day, this topic, this idea, this interaction different from what you and your audience have seen or read before? How will you develop this specific occasion, this story or scenario, so that it will be meaningful for both you and your audience?

2. *Use concrete, precise language and details.* Avoid abstract and trite language. Instead, use vivid and specific language that creates pictures and scenes in the minds of your readers. Also, use details that are significant and build to achieve your purpose.

3. *Carefully organize your narrative to achieve that purpose.* Consider what order or sequence of details is best to achieve an ending, dominant impression. What do you want your readers to think about after they finish reading your essay? What theme or images should linger in their minds? How will you build your narrative to achieve this single, final, prevailing impression?

4. *Use sensory details and figurative language to appeal to your audience's senses, involvedness, and emotions.* When you extend the literal meanings of words by appealing to the senses and intelligence of your audience through figures of speech such as allusions, metaphors, and similes, you allow for the possibility of deeper insights and new understandings, which will keep your readers intrigued. In essence, metaphors, similes, and allusions are comparisons. While, with metaphors and similes, the comparisons may not be exact or factually true, the objects, ideas, people, or actions compared share characteristics that range from basic similarity to arousing a far-reaching set of suggestions and associations that add richness to explanation and meaning. The comparison is more blatant with a simile; the writer or speaker uses "like" or "as" to make the comparison. The comparison with the metaphor is more subtle, implied.

Simile: His demeanor was as subtle as a missing front tooth.

Metaphor: I recognized the sign as soon as I met her. She was an arrow pointing upward, an unexpected detour, and I knew my road would surprisingly change.

Allusions are references typically to religious, literary, or historical figures, texts, or events. Allusions provide additional understanding or context to an author's purpose and message. They offer clues that invite us to interpret, participate, connect, and delve beyond the literal, textual surface.

Allusion: After the divorce he was single-minded, an Ahab, resolving to hurt her as much as she had hurt him.

5. *Show more, tell less.* Use strong active, not passive, verbs. Use concrete words and a sequence that simulates that of a moving camera. Insert dialogue if appropriate to create variety, sharper characterization, and a good pace to the narra-

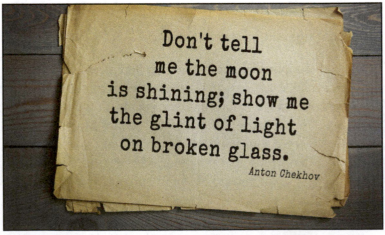

Don't tell me the moon is shining; show me the glint of light on broken glass.
Anton Chekhov

tive. Work to achieve, for your audience, a mental picture that conjures the characters, feelings, actions, and scenes (*showing*) rather than a summary or flat statement of the same (*telling*).

6. *End with a dominant image, action, or impression.* What resonates at the end for your audience? What are your readers thinking about? How have you planned for this dominant impression throughout your essay through the use of foreshadowing, imagery, characterization, action, or detail? This dominant image must align with your essay's purpose.

Read Scott Russell Sanders's "The Inheritance of Tools" and discuss how Sanders builds his descriptive narrative to evoke a dominant, resonating, single final impression.

The Inheritance of Tools

Scott Russell Sanders

At just about the hour when my father died, soon after dawn one February morning when ice coated the windows like cataracts, I banged my thumb with a hammer. Naturally I swore at the hammers the reckless thing, and in the moment of swearing I thought of what my father would say: "If you'd try hitting the nail it would go in a whole lot faster. Don't you know your thumb's not as hard as that hammer?" We both were doing carpentry that day, but far apart. He was building cupboards at my brother's place in Oklahoma; I was at home in Indiana, putting up a wall in the basement to make a bedroom for my daughter. By the time my mother called with news of his death—the long distance wires whittling her voice until it seemed too thin to bear the weight of what she had to say—my thumb was swollen. A week or so later a white scar in the shape of a crescent moon began to show above the cuticle and month by month it rose across the pink sky of my thumbnail. It took the better part of a year for the scar to disappear, and every time I noticed it I thought of my father.

The hammer had belonged to him, and to his father before him. The three of us have used it to build houses and barns and chicken coops, to upholster chairs and crack walnuts, to make doll furniture and bookshelves and jewelry boxes. The head is scratched and pockmarked, like an old plowshare that has been working rocky fields, and it gives off the sort of dull sheen you see on fast creek water in the shade. It is a finishing hammer, about the weight of a bread loaf, too light, really, for framing walls, too heavy for cabinet work, with a curved claw for pulling nails, a rounded head for pounding, a fluted neck for looks, and a hickory handle for strength.

The present handle is my third one, bought from a lumberyard in Tennessee, down the road from where my brother and I were helping my father build his retirement house. I broke the previous one by trying to pull sixteen-penny nails out of floor joists—a foolish thing to do with a finishing hammer, as my father pointed out. "You ever hear of a crowbar?" he said. No telling how many handles he and my grandfather had gone through before me. My grandfather used to cut down hickory trees on his farm, saw them into slabs, cure the planks in his hayloft, and carve handles with a drawknife. The grain in hickory is crooked and knotty and therefore tough, hard to split, like the grain in the two men who owned this hammer before me.

After proposing marriage to a neighbor girl, my grandfather used this hammer to build a house for his bride on a stretch of river bottom in northern Mississippi. The lumber for the place, like the hickory for the handle, was cut on his own land. By the day of the wedding he had not quite finished the house, and so right after the ceremony he took his wife home and put her to work. My grandmother had worn her Sunday dress for the wedding, with a fringe of lace tacked on around the hem in honor of the occasion. She removed this lace and folded it away before going out to help my grandfather nail siding on the house. "There she was in her good dress," he told me some forty odd years after that wedding day, "holding up them long pieces of clapboard while I hammered, and together we got the place covered up before dark." As the family grew to four, six, eight, and eventually thirteen, my grandfather used this hammer to enlarge his house room by room, like a chambered nautilus expanding its shell.

By and by the hammer was passed along to my father. One day he was up on the roof of our pony barn nailing shingles with it, when I stepped out the kitchen door to call him for supper. Before I could yell, something about the sight of him straddling the spine of that roof and swinging the hammer caught my eye and made me hold my tongue. I was five or six years old, and the world's commonplaces were still news to me. He would pull a nail from the pouch at his waist, bring the hammer down, and a moment later the thunk of the blow would reach my ears. And that is what had stopped me in my tracks and stilled my tongue, the momentary gap between seeing and hearing the blow. Instead of yelling from the kitchen door, I ran to the barn and climbed two rungs up the ladder-as far as I was allowed to go—and spoke quietly to my father. On our walk to the house he explained that sound takes time to make its way through air. Suddenly the world seemed larger, the air more dense, if sound could be held back like any ordinary traveler.

By the time I started using this hammer, at about the age when I discovered the speed of sound, it already contained houses and mysteries for me. The smooth handle was one my grandfather had made. In those days I needed both hands to swing it. My father would start a nail in a scrap of wood, and I would pound away until I bent it over.

"Looks like you got a hold of some of those rubber nails," he would tell me. "Here, let me see if I can find you some stiff ones." And he would rummage in a drawer until he came up with a fistful of more cooperative nails. "Look at the head," he would tell me. "Don't look at your hands, don't look at the hammer. Just look at the head of that nail and pretty soon you'll learn to hit it square."

Pretty soon I did learn. While he worked in the garage cutting dovetail joints for a drawer or skinning a deer or tuning an engine, I would hammer nails. I made innocent blocks of wood look like porcupines. He did not talk much in the midst of his tools, but he kept up a nearly ceaseless humming, slipping in and out of a dozen tunes in an afternoon, often running back over the same stretch of melody again and again, as if searching for a way out. When the humming did cease, I knew he was faced with a task requiring great delicacy or concentration, and I took care not to distract him.

He kept scraps of wood in a cardboard box—the ends of two-by-fours, slabs of shelving and plywood, odd pieces of molding—and everything in it was fair game. I nailed scraps together to fashion what I called boats or houses, but the results usually bore only faint resemblance to the visions I carried in my head. I would hold up these constructions to show my father, and he would turn them over in his hands admiringly, speculating about what they might be. My cobbled-together guitars might have been alien spaceships, my barns might have been models of Aztec temples, each wooden contraption might have been anything but what I had set out to make.

UNLEARNING AND RELEARNING: A Guide to College Composition

Now and again I would feel the need to have a chunk of wood shaped or shortened before I riddled it with nails, and I would clamp it in a vise and scrape at it with a handsaw. My father would let me lacerate the board until my arm gave out, and then he would wrap his hand around mine and help me finish the cut, showing me how to use my thumb to guide the blade, how to pull back on the saw to keep it from binding, how to let my shoulder do the work.

"Don't force it," he would say, "just drag it easy and give the teeth a chance to bite." As the saw teeth bit down, the wood released its smell, each kind with its own fragrance, oak or walnut or cherry or pine—usually pine because it was the softest, easiest for a child to work. No matter how weathered and gray the board, no matter how warped and cracked, inside there was this smell waiting, as of something freshly baked. I gathered every smidgen of sawdust and stored it away in coffee cans, which I kept in a drawer of the workbench. When I did not feel like hammering nails, I would dump my sawdust on the concrete floor of the garage and landscape it into highways and farms and towns, running miniature cars and trucks along miniature roads. Looming as huge as a colossus, my father worked over and around me, now and again bending down to inspect my work, careful not to trample my creations. It was a landscape that smelled dizzyingly of wood. Even after a bath my skin would carry the smell, and so would my father's hair, when he lifted me for a bedtime hug.

I tell these things not only from memory but also from recent observation, because my own son now turns blocks of wood into nailed porcupines, dumps cans full of sawdust at my feet and sculpts highways on the floor. He learns how to swing a hammer from the elbow instead of the wrist, how to lay his thumb beside the blade to guide a saw, how to tap a chisel with a wooden mallet, how to mark a hole with an awl before starting a drill bit. My daughter did the same before him, and even now, on the brink of teenage aloofness, she will occasionally drag out my box of wood scraps and carpenter something. So I have seen my apprenticeship to wood and tools reenacted in each of my children, as my father saw his own apprenticeship renewed in me.

The saw I use belonged to him, as did my level and both of my squares, and all four tools had belonged to his father. The blade of the saw is the bluish color of gun barrels, and the maple handle, dark from the sweat of hands, is inscribed with curving leaf designs. The level is a shaft of walnut two feet long, edged with brass and pierced by three round windows in which air bubbles float in oil-filled tubes of glass. The middle window serves for testing if a surface is horizontal, the others for testing if a surface is plumb or vertical. My grandfather used to carry this level on a gun rack behind the seat in his pickup, and when I rode with him I would turn around to watch the bubbles dance. The larger of two squares is called a framing square, a flat steel elbow, so beat up and tarnished you can barely make out the rows of numbers that show how to figure the cuts on rafters. The smaller one is called a try square, for marking right angles, with a blued steel blade for the shank and a brass-faced block of cherry for the head.

I was taught early on that a saw is not to be used apart from a square: "If you're going to cut a piece of wood," my father insisted, "you owe it to the tree to cut it straight." ‑morals

Long before studying geometry, I learned there is a mystical virtue in right angles. There is an unspoken morality in seeking the level and the plumb. A house will stand, a table will bear weight, the sides of a box will hold together, only if the joints are square and the members upright. When the bubble is lined up between two marks etched in the glass tube of a level, you have aligned yourself with the forces that hold the universe together. When you miter the corners of a picture frame each angle must be exactly forty-five degrees, as they are in the perfect triangles of Pythagoras, not a degree more or less. Otherwise the frame will hang crookedly, as if ashamed of itself and of its maker. No matter if the joints you are cutting do not show. Even if you are butting two pieces of wood together inside a cabinet, where no one except a wrecking crew will ever see them, you must take pains to ensure that the ends are square and the studs are plumb.

I took pains over the wall I was building on the day my father died. Not long after that wall was finished—paneled with tongue-and-groove boards of yellow pine, the nail holes filled with putty and the wood all stained and sealed—I came close to wrecking it one afternoon when my daughter ran howling up the stairs to announce that her gerbils had escaped from their cage and were hiding in my brand new wall. She could hear them scratching and squeaking behind her bed. "Impossible!" I said. "How on earth could they get inside my drum-tight wall?" "Through the heating vent," she answered. I went downstairs, pressed my ear to the honey-colored wood, and heard the *scritch, scritch* of tiny feet. "What can we do?" my daughter wailed. "They'll starve to death, they'll die of thirst, they'll suffocate.

"Hold on," I soothed. "I'll think of something."

While I thought and she fretted, the radio on her bedside delivered us the headlines: Several thousand people had died in a city in India from a poisonous cloud that had leaked overnight from a chemical plant. A nuclear-powered submarine had been launched. Rioting continued in South Africa. An airplane had been hijacked in the Mediterranean. Authorities calculated that several thousand homeless people slept on the sheets within sight of the Washington Monument. I felt my usual helplessness in the face of all these calamities. But here was my daughter, weeping because her gerbils were holed up in a wall. This calamity I could handle.

"Don't worry," I told her. "We'll set food and water by the heating vent and lure them out. And if that doesn't do the trick, I'll tear the wall apart until we find them.

She stopped crying and gazed at me. "You'd really tear it apart? Just for my gerbils? The wall?" Astonishment slowed her only for a second, however, before she ran to the workbench and began tugging at drawers, saying, "Let's see, what'll we need? Crowbar. Hammer. Chisels. I hope we don't have to use them—but just in case."

We didn't need the wrecking tools. I never had to assault my handsome wall, because the gerbils eventually came out to nibble at a dish of popcorn. But for several hours I studied the tongue-and-groove skin I had nailed up on the day of my father's death considering where to begin prying. There were no gaps in that wall, no crooked joints.

I had botched a great many pieces of wood before I mastered the right angle with a saw, botched even more before I learned to miter a joint. The knowledge of these things resides in my hands and eyes and the web work of muscles, not in the tools. There are machines for sale—powered miter boxes and radial-arm saws, for instance—that will enable any casual soul to cut proper angles in boards. The skill is invested in the gadget instead of the person who uses it, and this is what distinguishes a machine from a tool. If I had to earn my keep by making furniture or building houses, I suppose I would buy powered saws and pneumatic nailers; the need for speed would drive me to it. But since I carpenter only for my own pleasure or to help neighbors or to remake the house around the ears of my family, I stick with hand tools. Most of the ones I own were given to me by my father who also taught me how to wield them. The tools in my workbench are a double inheritance, for each hammer and level and saw is wrapped in a cloud of knowing.

All of these tools are a pleasure to look at and to hold. Merchants would never paste signs on them in stores. Their designs are old because they work, because they serve their purpose well. Like folk songs and aphorisms and the grainy bits of language, these tools have been pared down to essentials. I look at my claw hammer, the distillation of a hundred generations of carpenters, and consider that it holds up well beside those other classics-Greek vases, Gregorian chants Don Quixote, barbed fish hooks, candles, spoons. Knowledge of hammering stretches back to the humans who squatted beside fires, chipping flints. Anthropologists have a lovely name for those un-worked rocks that served as the earliest hammers. "Dawn stones," they are called. Their only qualification for the work, aside from hardness, is that they fit the hand. Our ancestors used them for grinding corn, tapping awls, smashing bones. From dawn stones to this claw hammer is a great leap in time, but no great distance in design or imagination.

On that iced-over February morning when I smashed my thumb with the hammer, I was down in the basement framing the wall that my daughter's gerbils would later hide in. I was thinking of my father, as I always did whenever I built anything, thinking how he would have gone about the work, hearing in memory what he would have said about the wisdom of hitting the nail instead of my thumb. I had the studs and plates nailed together all square and trim, and was lifting the wall into place when the phone rang upstairs. My wife answered, and in a moment she came to the basement door and called down softly to me. The stillness in her voice made me drop the framed wall and hurry upstairs. She told me my father was dead. Then I heard the details over the phone from my mother. Building a set of cupboards for my brother in Oklahoma, he had knocked off work early the previous afternoon because of cramps in his stomach. Early this morning, on his way into the kitchen of my brother's trailer, maybe going for a glass of water, so early that no one else was awake, he slumped down on the linoleum and his heart quit.

For several hours I paced around inside my house, upstairs and down, in and out of every room, looking for the right door to open and knowing there was no such door. My wife and children followed me and wrapped me in arms and backed away again, circling and staring as if I were on fire. Where was the door, the doors the door? I kept wondering. My smashed thumb turned purple and throbbed, making me furious. I wanted to cut it off and rush outside and scrape away at the snow and hack a hole in the frozen earth and bury the shameful thing.

I went down into the basement, opened a drawer in my workbench, and stared at the ranks of chisels and knives. Oiled and sharp, as my father would have kept them, they gleamed at me like teeth. I took up a clasp knife, pried out the longest blade and tested the edge on the hair of my forearm. A tuft came away cleanly and I saw my father testing the sharpness of tools on his own skin, the blades of axes and knives and gouges and hoes, saw the red hair shaved of in patches from his arms and the backs of his hands. "That will cut bear," he would say. He never cut a bear with his blades, now my blades, but he cut deer, dirt, wood. I closed the knife and put it away. Then I took up the hammer and went back to work on my daughter's wall, snugging the bottom plate against a chalk line on the floor, shimming the top plate against the joists overhead, plumbing the studs with my level, making sure before I drove the first nail that every line was square and true.

Discussion Questions

1. Analyze Sanders' theme of inheritance throughout the essay. In what ways is this more than an essay about the handing down, from one generation to another, of hammers and tools? What, exactly, has been inherited? How do you know? Where are you explicitly told what has been handed down, and where do you understand what has been handed down due to what you have been shown instead of directly told?

2. How does Sanders convey the passage of time? Look closely at his references to the accomplishments of his and our ancestors, the "speed of sound", "long distance wires," the generations of his family. How does the time motif contribute to the central theme of inheritance?

3. Locate the strong sensory images and metaphors Sanders uses throughout the essay. How do these images add a depth of knowing and feeling? How do they contribute to an additional layer of meaning? How do they increase audience engagement? Besides houses, coops, walls, barns, and furniture, what else, metaphorically, has Sanders' hammer allowed him to build?

4. Describe the structure of the essay. How does Sanders' preoccupation with carpentry detail and the "virtue of right angles" mirror his precision in constructing an essay? Refer specifically to his circular structure, narrative sequence, and deliberate, concrete diction.

5. Why does Sanders mention the day's radio headlines after his daughter informs him of the trapped gerbils? How does this paragraph contribute to his characterization and to his relationship with his daughter?

6. Some may disagree as to what section of this narrative resonates as the emotional center. What section, for you, is the emotional center? How does character development contribute to what and how you feel? Look, particularly, at what Sanders chooses to show in his interactions with his father and with his daughter.

7. Look closely at how "The Inheritance of Tools" begins and ends. What narrative strategies does Sanders use to engage his audience at the onset? How and why does his last sentence resonate with his audience? What was foreshadowed or "built" into the essay to create this final, dominant impression?

8. Locate the allusions in the essay. How do these references add a depth of meaning and purpose?

9. What, specifically, is meaningful to you? What would you do, in a descriptive essay, to make what is meaningful to you meaningful for your audience?

First-year college student, John Connor Oliverio, describes where he finds meaning in his essay "Puff."

Puff

John Connor Oliverio

I've been a cigar smoker for over a year now, and the roots of that leaf are buried deep into my family's tradition. My lineage is Italian through and through. We all do stereotypical Italian things like talk with our hands, and eat spaghetti with a fork and spoon. We sit around and talk for hours long after the buttery noodles and the marinara were devoured. My parents and my grandma love wine. My grandmother swirls the wine around to aerate it and after she sips her white Moscato, she smirks. We are all devout Roman Catholics and attend church every Sunday. I had a bootlegging Mafia member as a great great-grandfather. He came from Italy with his family and had nothing. Then, according to the dinner table story, one day a red car dashed into his driveway and he appeared, a handsome Italian man in a nice suit and a cigar in his hand. My family members soon discovered that he not only bootlegged, but they also found a baseball bat in his trunk with the same shade of blood red as the car.

The men in my family have an affinity for cigars, and they wanted me to partake in the tradition of smoking. I remember the first cigar my dad presented to me. It was a Camacho cigar wrapped in a thin layer of plastic to help keep in the humidity. Its lovely light brown, tightly wrapped Connecticut style leaf was not at all what I imagined. I was expecting a nice dark brown almost black cigar like the ones you see in the mob boss movies. My dad unwrapped the cigars, one for me and one for him. He sniffed it. A slow grin stretched all the way across his bearded face.

He then handed me the cigar and gestured for me to do the same. The fragrance of the leaf's tobacco filled my head with splendor as I waited for my smoke that night. My father cut the cigars with his cigar cutter then proceeded to light his cigar. I struck my match, the flame glowing bright reddish orange; but for some reason, I struggled to light my cigar. My father leaned over me and, together, we lit the cigar. He immediately instructed me that you never inhale the cigar smoke. You simply puff. "When you puff on a cigar, he said, "you suck in like you're drinking from a straw, without the swallowing part. And exhale to push the smoke out of your mouth."

I followed his direction. The hot smoke rushed into my mouth, filling it with a smooth rich taste, almost like eating your first candy bar. As I exhaled, I watched the smoke leave my mouth. As it rose, the white smoke matched the moon's glow. "Well, how was it?" my father asked. "Fantastic," I said. We sat down on the swing and began to chat, father and son stuff. My mother came outside to join us and to my surprise, she stole my dad's cigar and took a few puffs. I remember that when my grandfather used to watch me play outside he'd be smoking a cigar, and my uncle would also be smoking a cigar when I went to visit him. Just about every male person in my family smoked a cigar. My father that night told me that when you smoke a cigar you just relax and just enjoy life, as God wanted you to.

After that day my high school friends and I started to smoke cigars regularly. My shy friend became much more confident afterwards and actually asked a girl, whom he was falling for, on a date. She said no. We would go down to the fields by my house and we lit up under a pavilion and just enjoy ourselves for an hour or two. When we were about halfway done, the smoke grew thick and covered the majority of the pavilion. We sat there in deep thought, deep smoke, just enjoying the company of others, swapping cigars, testing all the different flavors. The scent of the Java Drew Estate cigar was a fine coffee chocolate mix, and it tasted like the real thing, too. Other times we would sit and talk for hours—talk about our soccer season; rehash old stories about each other; talk about girls; and just hangout.

I came to college assuming I would be the only one who enjoys the classy, and sophisticated, cigar. One day, while walking back to my dorm, I smelled the sweet scent of a cigar, and realized that the man smoking it was my neighbor. When I approached him, he led me into his room. He presented me with a nice wooden box that was well taken care of. I opened it and saw a forest of cigars. Apparently, at my college, a group of guys hung around and smoked cigars and laughed and just had a good time as I had with my high school friends. I attended one of their meetings, a Newman Club meeting. One of the guys I befriended smoked a pipe. "The manliest of men smoke a pipe and the richest of men smoke cigars," he repeated. I eventually bought myself a pipe. The fine craftsmanship of the laminate wood covered the brown bowl while the smooth black filter rested, just waiting to have smoke rushed through it. My fire time with the pipe was relatively the same as with the cigar. The taste was quite smooth, but with a twist. The fragrance of pipe tobacco is mesmerizingly sweet. The smell was like being in a field of one thousand of your favorite scented candles or like smelling a hundred of your favorite flowers. I still preferred cigars, but my new friend had a point; they are more expensive. The sweet draw of a cigar fills your mouth with a tangy spice, or a rich creamy taste, or a more bitter taste. You can even find some cigars that taste like cheesecake if you look hard enough. You'll get your money's worth.

I brought my pipe to my parents' home in North Carolina over Thanksgiving break. Again, we did all the usual, stereotypical family things my Italian family did over the holidays; we cooked, and then ate until we felt we could explode. After dinner, my dad walked over to the kitchen counter and pulled out two cigars. The ring of the cigars was orange and brown with an angry and powerful bull on it. Three other colors, green, white and red, matched the Italian flag. The word "Maduro" was written as its title.

"I'll do you one better," I said to my father. I showed him my pipe. I set it on the table, angling it up with a little wooden prop.

"I've never smoked a pipe," my father said. "What's it like?" I unwrapped the tobacco bag and held it under my father's now. The smell of unlit tobacco made my father salivate. "It's similar to smoking a cigar," I said, "but more for the aroma than the overall taste." I took a small pinch and placed it into the bowl of the pipe, then from my pipe bag I grabbed this shiny metal object with a flat piece, a pointy piece, and a scoop piece.

"What's that?" my father asked "A pipe packing tool," I said. I used the flat part to gently push the tobacco into the bowl like a potter would do with a plant. I repeated this twice to fill up the pipe and pack it correctly. We took the cigars and the pipe outside. The moon was full on a not so warm southern night. My father struck a match and struggled with the leaf to get it lit. I leaned close to him. "Here, let me help," I said. I took the pipe and lit a match, placed the flame onto the tobacco, and started puffing. The flame danced up and down as the pipe sucked the flame through the tobacco to the bottom of the bowl. A small fire emerged on the top of the bowl. The smoke rushed from the leaves through the mouthpiece of the pipe and into my mouth. The released smoke traveled upwards, disappearing in the moonlight.

I handed my father the pipe. "Here," I said. "Try it now." He took the pipe and took one, slow puff. I waited in anticipation. He took another puff, expelling the smoke from his mouth and drawing new smoke in. He then drew one long one after expelling his previous puff.

"How was it?" I asked. His beard rose as he grinned. "Fantastic," he said. For a long time we sat and talked, father to son, son to father, until we puffed the tobacco to ash.

Discussion Questions

1. Describe the effect of Oliverio's opening two sentences. Look closely at his language.

2. Describe Oliverio's interplay between what is stereotypical about his family and his experiences and what is not. How does the structure of his narrative—in particular, his opening and ending sequences—contribute to the meaning of his essay and to its dominant impression?

3. Describe the sensory imagery of "Puff" and how this imagery evokes audience interest and participation.

4. What is meaningful to Oliverio? How do you know? Does he come right out and tell you, or do you feel what is meaningful because of what he shows?

In "Learning Perseverance," first-year composition student Macy Cain poignantly describes what she has learned from her brother.

Learning Perseverance

Macy Cain

When I was six years old, two women came into my home. They wore the same attire—high waisted, dark colored pencil skirts, and prescription glasses shielding their eyes like windows, aiding their sense of sight as they observed my brother. Their hair was perfectly slicked back into ponytails, as they clutched shiny black clipboards with freshly manicured hands. They fixated their focus on my brother like a dog watching a treat. They stared and wrote things down as he played with his toy trains the same as he did every day. He'd sit himself on the floor so his head was level with the surface of his train table, one eye squeezed shut, and the other glued to his favorite toy train, "Gordon," as he ran it along the tracks at a slow, consistent speed. The women saw this as abnormal, but it was normal to my family and me. If Clayton were anywhere, he was at his train table, running his trains along the tracks as he normally would. No one else could play with them or touch them, and if he was there playing, he didn't accept anyone joining him. He didn't mean anything by this—he just preferred to be alone.

After the women observed my brother, they talked to my mother for what seemed like forever, and that time my mother was the one staring and writing things down. Confused and concerned, her eyes snapped back and forth between my brother and the women as they explained autism spectrum disorder. She furrowed her brow and carved notes into a spiral notebook as quickly as she could question the women. My parents spent a lot of time together that day with my brother, just talking and watching Clayton play with his trains.

My sister and I were sitting on the couch watching TV, when my mother approached us with tall glasses of chocolate milk. She sat down at the table across from us in attempt to explain things. "I wanted to tell you girls why Mrs. Smith and Ms. Andrews were here today," she began. "They were here to help us figure out why Clayton has 'meltdowns.'" The expression on her face itself was an interrogation: she was searching for clues that showed we may be confused. "You girls know how sometimes when you want to play with Clay and he gets mad? Or how when we go somewhere noisy and he starts to cry?" We nodded our heads as if she were finally getting us to understand. "Ms. Andrews and Mrs. Smith showed us that Clayton's brain just works a little differently than ours do. There's nothing wrong with that; that's just what makes him not like loud noises or music, and have trouble talking. I know this might be hard for you guys to understand, but it's hard for Daddy and me to understand, too."

I looked at my older sister Ryley to see what she was going to say. I looked up to her a lot. She taught me how to cut our Barbie's hair at the "hair salon," create beds out of leaves for the "fairies" in our back yard, and how to make bubbles with straws in your drink at restaurants. My sister was all-knowing, and if ever I didn't know what to say or do, my sister would. I turned to her. "Will Ms. Andrews and Mrs. Smith help Clayton learn how to talk?" my sister asked. My mother's eyes began to glisten as she processed my sister's words. "I think so," my mom replied. My mother hugged us both at the same time, telling us how much she loves us before getting up, looking back, and then walking away.

By the time I was ten years old, I had watched my brother have "melt downs" on a regular basis. Usually it was in the morning, in my mother's attempt to get him dressed. He was six at this point, and he couldn't stand to wear clothes. My mother would wrestle him just to get his shirt on. He would scream and cry. If something was too loud, he would shout and cover his ears. If something smelled too strongly, he would cry and nearly throw up. If someone touched him or got too close for comfort, he would take off running, without looking back, not caring where he was headed—only for a way to resolve his discomfort. Sometimes my sister and I would watch and try to help, and we'd usually make sure that we had ourselves together and ready for school when she finally did get him dressed.

Although I wasn't directly affected by my brother's meltdowns, they took a toll on me. Sometimes it almost seemed that the three different therapy programs he was in wasn't helping. Processing his disability was difficult. It was like watching someone you love slowly being swallowed by a bubble—a giant bubble of discomfort and helplessness. One minute we would be chasing each other in the front yard, running as fast as our bodies could allow, and laughing like nothing bad in the world existed. Then suddenly, a motorcycle would drive past our house, roaring and gurgling like there was a humongous portable speaker attached to its engine, creating another bubble. He knew it was coming. The bubble would float to him, roll right on top of him, and entrap him. Fear would cloak the happiness that constructed his smile and sparkling eyes, and his brain would go into panic mode. H drew his hands to his ears and his mouth opened wide to let out a scream. "It's okay Clayton!" my sister and I would say over and over, even though we knew whatever we said to try to calm him would not help.

On rare occasion, my brother would relax. My mother would hold down my brother's arms and my dad his legs. My mother would say his name repeatedly, in a calming, soothing tone. Then finally, she sucked in what seemed like a gallon of air. However, instead of screaming, she blew in my brother's face. Not like blowing out candles—all in one gust—but a slow, gentle breath; like a breeze you'd feel outside in the middle of spring, just when everything seemed to be still. When she'd blow on his face, the screaming would halt. His mouth, that seemed drawn open by metal clamps, would shut. The tenseness in his face and body would release and disintegrate, and my brother would become my brother again.

When I was 16 years old, I learned something from my brother. We were eating lunch together. He ate grilled cheese that my mother made; one of the few options he could bring himself to eat. He was happy and content, despite the morning he had, wrestling another bubble formed by lab work. We had the day off school to get this done and go to the doctor's; my mother never knew how long it would take. I sat and poked at my salad, thinking about my art project. The graphite piece of the Eiffel Tower seemed to bite at me like a mosquito since I started it. No matter how much I erased or blended, it never seemed to look right. It made me start to feel like the plan I had for my future in the fine arts was going down the toilet. Yet, my brother wasn't bothered by anything in that moment. He wasn't worried about the fact that he'd have to get bloodwork done again someday. The thought that he had to go to school tomorrow and read his book, which to him was more of an attempt to organize what looked like a jumbled mess of black letters on paper, never came to mind. He wasn't bothered by the idea that he would have to take a shower that night and not be able to know when the water was too hot for his skin. He was not at all bothered by his daily battles that most people don't have. Instead he sat there, chuckling, as he chewed a curved line into the crust that was left of his sandwich, and held it in front of his mouth like a smiley face to make me laugh.

When I was seventeen, I drove my brother to school for the first time. It was the first time in my life I had seen him going to school relaxed. It was the first time he had talked to me on our way to school. He wasn't motion sick from the bus. I took this morning for granted—my mind was too flooded with the stress of junior year to realize what was happening. At the red light, we were slumped in my rust orange, too-old-to-drive, Pontiac Sunfire, rain coating everything in existence and turning what could have been a bright summer sky to a dark, suffocating fog. I was nearly in tears, thinking about how much my life stinks. How I must take two AP tests in one day, go to volleyball practice after school, finish my art project before fifth period, and go to work on time. But there was my joyful brother, thankful that he won't be nauseated on his way to school, or uncomfortable from the noise on the bus.

© Macrovector/Shutterstock.com

I am eighteen years old. I am in an old classroom at La Roche College, standing before my art teacher and a few others from my class, getting ready to walk into a gym filled with a few hundred artists across the region, nominated for the same award as me. I think about my art project—how long it took me to complete, and how I'd try to mimic my brother's perseverance with every hour I put into the piece. I think about my brother, sitting in the giant stadium filled with one thousand people talking, laughing, eating cookies and fruit punch. I think about how my brother was years ago and how at that time, this would have made my stomach churn and my palms sweat. It makes me smile as I can picture him now, after everything he has gone through, smiling and laughing with my parents as everyone else would have been, although he probably still didn't like the noise. We all stand to line up, so we can formally walk into the facility and accept our awards. I smile, as I realize the window is open, and I feel a cool breeze brush my face.

Discussion Questions

1. In "Learning Perseverance," how does Cain develop her characters? What do you remember about her brother? What do you most recall about her mother? How does she make you feel for these family members?

2. What is the effect of Cain's last line? How was it foreshadowed?

3. What is the effect of the repeated bubble imagery in the essay?

4. Examine Cain's last paragraph. Notice the verb tense switch and the heightened focus on herself. How do these narrative strategies contribute to the dominant impression of the piece?

Writing Assignment

Now it is your turn to bring action and scenes to life. Make us feel the effect of a mother's gentle breath. Let us taste a cheesecake cigar, and witness a father's expelled, rising pipe smoke "disappearing in the moonlight." Invite us to feel the weight of what is meaningful to you—what is "square and true."

Using the above strategy tips for descriptive writing, write an essay in which you show more than tell what is meaningful to you. Create characters, images, and a narrative sequence that build to a single, dominant impression. Remember your audience. Make this essay intriguing for your reader, from your first few sentences to your closing words, so that we are invited to participate, witness, and feel in order to find meaning in your essay, also.

Chapter [11]

Argument Writing

Unlearning

1. Since arguments carry a negative connotation, and readers already have a set position on most topics, spending the time attempting to convince others, especially those who hold an opposing viewpoint, is a futile and thankless endeavor. Even those who agree with the writer's position stand to discover little since the writer is confirming or reinforcing what the reader already believes.

2. It is best to keep your point of view to yourself. In our current politically correct environment, saying how you feel can get you into trouble, or even fired.

Relearning

1. When you read critically, not only do you discern the strengths and flaws in the author's essay, but you begin to evaluate and rethink your own point of view. Critical analysis forces you to look at the logic, evidence, and persuasion for *both* sides of an issue, and then evaluate which side carries more weight. Some of your opinions have been formed simply from jumping on a bandwagon—a passive acceptance from what you have heard from authority figures, friends, advertisers, or someone you admire. Quite frankly, this is a lazy, and often dangerous, way to think. How can passive acceptance be dangerous? Individuals and groups persuade because they want something from you—your money, your vote, your

acquiescence. What happens when you so easily surrender you sovereignty, you opinion, to others? When you surrender your power, your ability to think and respond critically, others can then take advantage of you. When you become aware of manipulation, injustice, misrepresentation, bias, inequality, or any issue that, for you, is urgent and requires fair analysis and response, you may be compelled to write about it, to argue your points, and persuade others.

© Anna Tigra/Shutterstock.com

Since we often do not think about *how* we think, or *why* we think the way we think, writing arguments helps us to *focus* on the pertinent issues at hand—for *both sides* of the argument. Don't just don't present your point of view. Your argument must be balanced. A reader who accuses you of "stacking the deck" or bias may be less likely to listen to the merits of your argument. Presenting a fair, thorough counterargument will enable you and your reader to acknowledge the strengths and weaknesses of each side of the argument. Once you equally present your argument and the counterargument, you should then logically persuade your reader why you believe your point of view carries more weight. Expose the flaws, weaknesses, contradictions, or gaps in the counterclaim. Sometimes, through the processes of writing and researching, writers discover that their original point of view is flawed and that the counterargument is stronger. That should not be such a surprise for those who understand that writing is a process of learning and discovering—a process of unlearning and relearning and realizing what we had not previously known. Writing arguments, then, can help us be more fair thinkers and critics. When we respectfully acknowledge both sides of the argument, we do something critical that is often missing today in the art of

persuasion: we present a welcoming tone that is not dismissive, but one that encourages deliberation, discussion, debate, and further dialogue. When our narrative and verbal voices and tones encourage our audience to listen and consider instead of instantly defend and react, we are more likely to be heard.

© Monkey Business Images/Shutterstock.com

2. While it is true that you are discouraged or even reprimanded from presenting your point of view

about certain topics in a setting such as the workplace, you should feel free to candidly and politely exchange ideas at your college or university. The term "liberal arts" itself connotes a free exchange of ideas, open communication, and effective argumentation that leads to clear thinking and problem solving. If you cannot talk about issues in a liberal arts college, then where are you free to discuss them? Again, considering and weighing all points of view ultimately makes your perspective more balanced, fair, and heard. Once you have mastered the art of arguing logically and considering multiple points of view, then you will have confidence in the art of gentle yet candid persuasion, both to those in and out of the university setting, which includes presenting your informed point of view to those who may have a lot to learn from you.

Now that you have become a better critical reader by more astutely assessing and responding to the works of others (Chapter 9), you have the tools to construct your own analysis and response to your chosen topic, to build your own solid argument. Consider the components of the argument.

Parts of An Argument

Intellectuals and educators classify the parts of an argument in their own ways, with their own vocabulary. In this chapter, you will be presented with four parts that serve more as umbrella terms with several sub-components.

Part #1

The Claim

In an essay, the claim is the statement that presents your position or stance on an issue. Therefore, in an academic paper such as an argumentative writing, the claim is your thesis statement. The thesis statement consists of three very important components that come together to effectively present your position or stance on an issue. The first component is the topic, or the name of the issue, being discussed. The second component is your opinion, or stance, on the issue. Finally, you provide your main reasons or criteria as to why your opinion is true. These reasons or criteria are also known as the divisions of proof. However, presenting the three components of a thesis statement is only part of the puzzle.

Like any builder, you will have to finetune your construction over time. At first, you will compose a preliminary thesis statement, but it will likely need work as time goes on. In other words, as you revise your paper you will also revise your thesis. For a student, this can be difficult because you might not know exactly what it is you need to do in order to revise it. The following is a detailed checklist of the dos and don'ts in regards to writing and revising thesis statements.

THE DON'TS

1. Do not try to cram two or three topics into one thesis. Do not be too broad. Be focused.

Cramming two or more topics into a thesis essentially means you will need to write two or more papers, and when a thesis is too broad, you cannot properly argue your thesis within the assigned length of the paper.

New automobiles have several major flaws, and many consumers cannot afford to purchase them.

2. Do not use vague and abstract word choice that has no meaning. Be specific.

The problem with vague and abstract words is that they are unclear and could mean different things to different readers. (Example words include "negative," "positive," "people," and "society.")

EXAMPLE

Excessive corporate tax rates have a negative impact on society.

3. Do not use generalized word choice that oversimplifies a complex argument.

The problem with using generalized words is that they ignore the limitations of your argument and are so absolute that they push your claim into being a logical fallacy. (Example words include "all," "none," "not," "only," "every," "always," and "never.")

EXAMPLE

The death penalty should never be an option in our society.

4. Do not make announcements. Do not tell the reader.

The reader already knows you wrote the paper because your name is on it. The focus of the paper should be on your topic, not you. In addition, academic writing such as the argument is typically written in third person.

EXAMPLE

In this paper, I will discuss why we must save the environment.

5. Do not report a fact as a thesis.

Facts are not arguable. Thesis statements are.

EXAMPLE

Some people have snakes as pets.

THE DOS

1. Be Concise: A thesis should have a single, limited, and narrow focus.

2. Be Clear: A thesis should have specific and appropriate word choice.

3. Be Analytic: A thesis should reveal your position to the reader

The previous section provided example errors in thesis writing. Now, take a look at how to correct some of those errors using the guidance of being concise, clear, and analytic.

EXAMPLE (Original): Excessive corporate tax rates have a negative impact on society.

EXAMPLE (Revised): Excessive corporate tax rates make U.S. businesses less attractive than those of global competitors.

EXAMPLE (Original): The death penalty should never be an option in our society.

EXAMPLE (Revised): The death penalty is an inadequate deterrent to crime in the United States.

EXAMPLE (Original): In this paper, I will discuss why we must save the environment.

EXAMPLE (Revised): To ensure a future with cleaner air to breathe, Americans must put forth more effort to preserve the environment by using energy-efficient technology.

Part #2

The Evidence

Quality evidence can be classified into two categories: primary and secondary sources. Primary sources are first-hand information and can consist of original documentation such as transcripts, personal diaries or journals, interviews, speeches, law and government documents, original art and literature, and finally any publication providing new content such as a newspaper or scholarly journal's original reporting. Meanwhile, secondary sources are a response to primary sources. They are a synthesis, interpretation, and commentary of what already exists, and they are not new and original like primary sources. Although primary and secondary sources are very different in nature, they can exist within the same form of media such as newspapers, scholarly journals, and others. However, secondary sources include additional forms of media such as textbooks, encyclopedias, dictionaries, biographies, and dissertations.

Part #3

The Qualifiers

Even though you have a thesis and claim it to be true, you have to understand that your claim or point of view is not a universal truth. Exceptions and/or alternatives exist. After all, that is why your argument is debatable. That is why people can disagree on the issue. Therefore, it is important that you consider the limitations and boundaries of your position. A qualifier is a word or phrase that provides a limitation or degree to your claim (thesis). In other words, qualifiers provide the conditions (who, what, when, where, why, and how) for your thesis to be true and help prevent writers from falling into a logical fallacy like a hasty generalization. The following charts provide a list of sample qualifier words and phrases that can help writers.

Qualifier Words
Basically, Many, Most, Mostly, May, Might, Probably, Possibly, Likely, Unlikely, Improbable, Rarely, Infrequently, Few, Doubtful, Seldom, Sporadically, Usually, Repeatedly, Sometimes, Some, Numerous, Countless, Virtually

Qualifier Phrases
For a long time, May be, May have been, Might have been, A majority, For a long time, Not many, A small number, A minority, Hardly any

In order to completely understand how using absolute words and qualifier words affect the presentation of your argument and the meaning of your writing, take a look at the following example:

EXAMPLE (Initially using absolutes): Dan's measurements are always accurate.

EXAMPLE (Revised using qualifiers): Dan's measurements are probably accurate.

As you can see, there is a difference in the two sentences. The first sentence uses the absolute word "always" and implies that Dan's measurements are incapable of error, whereas the second sentences uses the qualifier word "probably" and implies that Dan's measurements have historically been correct but acknowledges that people, even Dan, can make a mistake.

While using qualifiers exemplifies great responsibility, it is possible for writers to overuse qualifiers which may cause a paper to be unclear. For students, three of the most commonly overused qualifiers are "a lot," "really," and "very." The following examples demonstrate how qualifiers can be overused and how they can be fixed:

EXAMPLE (Overused Qualifier): During this time of the year, the weather is very different.

EXAMPLE (Revised): During this time of the year, the weather is freezing.

Often, when writers cannot find the right words to convey what they want to say, they will select a generic or ineffective word to substitute, and the word is usually accompanied by one of the overused qualifiers. In the example above, this phenomenon is demonstrated with the use of "very different," which doesn't capture the specificity expressed by the corrected term "freezing." Take a look at one more example:

EXAMPLE (Overused Qualifier): Mr. Johnson provided some really important information in class.

EXAMPLE (Revised): Mr. Johnson presented surprising state demographic trends during class.

The example above overuses the qualifiers "some really" and pairs them with the generic term "important." Then, the sentence was corrected by replacing those words with the more specific, defined words. In both examples, you can see that the revised sentences provide the reader with a more precise, clear understanding.

Part 4

The Audience

There are so many ways to profile an audience. You can classify your audience by socioeconomic status, political affiliation, geographical region, gender, and age, as well as by the many other classifications that exist. However, with writing, as with any form of communication, there are senders and receivers. A single classification of audience can only be taken so far. Overlaps exist.

For instance, your target audience may be women, but women, obviously live in very different areas throughout the world. What might be true of a woman in urban New York City might not be true of a woman in rural Indiana because their priorities, values, interests, and backgrounds may differ.

You may think of your audience in more simplistic terms: those who agree with you, those who disagree with you, or those who are neutral regarding the issue you're discussing in your writing. Are you writing to those who already agree with you in order to further provide evidence and sources to bolster your shared claim? Are you writing to persuade a hostile audience who disagrees with you? Or are you writing to persuade a neutral audience to not only care about an issue but to also agree with your side of the issue by the end of your paper?

Structure of an Argument

Now that you are familiar with the parts of the argument, it is important to know where they go in a paper, or better yet, how they can be used. However, it is important to point out that there is no one way to present an argument. It is very much situational, and you need to be the best judge you can be in determining your purpose and audience. For instance, are you dealing with an audience that is familiar with this topic or an audience that is not? Analyzing your situation and asking such a question are important because it will help you determine whether you need background information in the introduction or not, and if you do, how much you will need to provide to the reader. In general, background information familiarizes your reader about your topic and sets up your argument. Even those familiar with the topic may appreciate reminders or additional information they had not heard or read before. Sometimes, however, providing background information in the introduction, regardless if the audience is knowledgeable or not, could have unintended consequences. Knowledgeable readers might feel belittled or bored with what they are reading, and in turn, they will become disengaged. When it comes to persuasion, you try to get an audience engaged and motivated, so, at times, uncritically including background information in the introduction could produce the opposite effect of what you may have intended. That is why you need to familiarize yourself with your readers.

Previously, you have learned that there are three sections to an essay: the introduction, the body, and the conclusion. You will be presented with each of the three sections of an essay and how the parts of an argument can be inserted into each section. Please keep in mind that the majority of your paper should be written with your own original words. As a writer, your job is to present your position on an issue, and the evidence and sources you find are added to back up your position, not vice versa. In general, your argument should approximately be 70% your own words and 30% supporting evidence to back up your words.

The evidence that you supply in your paper will need to be governed by a proper citation method, and the subject of the class you are taking in college matters a great deal in determining which citation method is acceptable. For instance, any subject that falls under the humanities discipline would use the MLA (Modern Language Association) citation format, so your English papers will likely be using the MLA citation format. However, you might encounter other citation formats in an English class, and one of the likely reasons for using a different citation format will be the instructor teaching you different ways to properly cite sources. The APA (American Psychological Association) citation format is typically used in any subject that falls under the science and business disciplines.

The Introduction

The introduction is very important to a paper. For starters, it is where you introduce yourself to the reader, and first impressions matter. Your tone as well as your writing style will be on display, so you will want to make them appealing to readers, especially when your goal is to try and persuade them to share your position.

Another purpose of the introduction is to present your topic as well as your stance on the topic. The topic of your paper will likely be clearly stated for your reader toward the very beginning. Shortly after, you should include your stance in a well-written thesis statement. The thesis traditionally appears toward the end of the introduction, usually as the last sentence.

Finally, the introduction is an olive branch to the reader, an invitation to what you have written, but the reader is far more important than one might think. Because writing is a form of communication, it requires senders and receivers to do what is expected of them in order for the communication to be effective. Each side shares a responsibility in communication. Because you are the writer, you assume the role as a sender, and as a sender, your goal is to persuade the reader to share your position by the end of the paper, as mentioned earlier. However, who are these receivers, these members of your audience?

Building bridges to the audience you are trying to reach is essential to being successful in persuading them. One technique that some writers use to reach out to a hostile or opposing audience is to acknowledge an understanding of their points of view in the introduction. It sends a message to the opposing side that you are aware of their position and even potentially builds your credibility as a writer in their eyes. Providing common ground as well as showing empathy or respect to their position can help even more.

Neutral readers are those who have no intellectual or emotional investment in the issue you are discussing in your paper. They neither agree nor disagree with you. As a writer, your job is to make them care, so you need to address the questions as to why readers should care about this issue as well as the position being presented. You need to make it personal to them. Emotional appeals, or pathos, and a sense of urgency may help here. You need to explain how your topic matters and affects their lives. Next, you need to consider why your position is the correct one. Be fair and respectful by presenting the alternative perspectives. Doing so will also build your credibility as a writer, and the introduction is a great place to inform the audience of this important background information.

Finally, reaching out to a reader who already agrees with you could be the most difficult task. To them, what you are writing might seem redundant. Therefore, when writing to those who already agree with you, it important that you make your paper worthy of their time. One of the best ways of doing that would be to write a new, fresh perspective the reaffirms the position, or to include sources and support for your position that bolsters the shared position of your audience. Make sure, however, that your position is arguable and you are not writing about that same old topic with the same pieces of evidence that your audience has heard many times before. Some instructors even forbid students to write about certain topics for this very reason. Remember, for you, writing should be an opportunity to discover, unlearn, and relearn. If you are simply writing about what you already know, and what your audience has already heard, both you and your audience will not be engaged or inspired.

Depending on the length of your assignment, the introduction can be anywhere from a single paragraph to several paragraphs. In shorter writing assignments, you will likely have to accomplish everything that has been discussed in a single paragraph. For longer papers that are 8-10 pages or more, it is likely you will have multiple paragraphs for the introduction due to the amount and depth of content required.

The Body

The body of the paper is the most essential part because it is where you argue the reasons or criteria (the divisions of proof) that are presented in your claim (thesis). To make your paper consistent, the reasons or criteria should be presented in the exact same order as they appear in the claim, and each reason should be backed up with supporting evidence. Without evidence, the claim you are making is essentially pointless. Furthermore, it is important to understand that the quantity of the evidence you provide matters as much as the quality.

Quantity matters because it is entirely possible that you will not satisfy the readers with enough evidence to prove your point. Furthermore, readers with a negative or neutral stance to your own will require more evidence than those who share your position. It is vital that you provide enough details and evidence to explain your position as well as counter potential rebuttals. When conducting initial research, you can never have too much evidence. The more evidence you have, the better, but there will come a time before writing when you need to determine how much evidence is enough. *Remember, rebuttal after the counterargument is essential in order to turn your audience's attention back to your point of view and to the solid evidence you have provided. Here, in the rebuttal, show the gaps, contradictions, weaknesses, flawed evidence, lack of representative samples or anecdotes, dated information, and flaws in logic in order to dilute what appeared to be some of the strong points in the counterclaims.* Your job in your argument is that of persuasion. In the rebuttal, you are showing, in a variety of ways, why you are convinced that your perspective is stronger than that of your opponents

Quality of evidence matters because it is entirely possible that the evidence you provide is not strong enough to persuade readers to see your point of view, so out of all of the evidence you have collected, you will need to determine what evidence is the most persuasive. You will likely do this in conjunction with determining how much evidence is enough. In other words, quality will likely be the standard of what evidence makes it into the paper and what does not. When you evaluate your evidence for quality, the word you should think of is "representative." Ask yourself if the evidence backs your claim, or is representative of the claim. Representative evidence is not distorted by bias or emotion. It is objective and free of emotion. While anecdotal evidence (stories and personal interviews) can be persuasive and use emotion to reach an audience, you need objective evidence. Representative evidence usually consists of facts and statistics that can stem from a variety of sources such as studies and research. However, there is more to the body than just providing good, quality evidence in support of your position.

Always remember that you are trying to sell your position to the reader. Therefore, you will have to heavily consider your audience. You will need to fulfill the expectations of your introduction by considering your purpose and the audience you are trying to reach. Additionally, you should include necessary background information when discussing certain points because some readers will likely need it to understand what you are trying to say. Furthermore, remember to fairly address potential objections and other points of view (never ignore potential opposition) when writing about certain points.

Much like the introduction, the length of the body depends on the length of the assignment. For shorter writing assignments, you will likely devote one paragraph discussing each reason or criterion in the body while longer writing assignments will require you to devote multiple paragraphs for each one. Should you have to devote multiple paragraphs to a single reason or criterion, think of ways in which you can divide the information into subcategories.

The Conclusion

You always want to conclude with strength. The conclusion is your last chance to make an impression on the reader, so you must take it seriously. While so many textbooks and instructors simply focus on summarizing the main points of your position and restating the thesis, a conclusion must be considered for so much more. It should be so impactful and unforgettable that the reader is left thinking about what you have written. Therefore, like the introduction, the conclusion should have great focus on the audience, the reader.

In order to greatly impact the reader and to move past mere summary, you can incorporate the following into your conclusion: a relevant and inspirational quote by a noted personality, a call to action, a recommendation or potential solution, an example or anecdote illustrating a key point, a metaphor or image that resonates on a deeper level, or a rhetorical question. While most of these are pretty self-explanatory, the concept of a rhetorical question in a conclusion needs further elaboration.

First, it is important to understand that the generic purpose of a conclusion is to end a paper. Asking traditional questions usually requires answers, so including traditional questions in a conclusion may defeat the purpose of what you are trying to do in a conclusion, which is to end your paper. However, rhetorical questions are perfect for conclusions because the answer to the question is obvious or known. They are also used to create a dramatic effect, so when one of the goals of a conclusion is to impact the reader beyond the paper, rhetorical questions serve even more of a purpose in concluding an argumentative paper.

The Citation of Sources

As mentioned earlier in the chapter, the discipline, the subject, determines what citation style you will use for your college writing. In a college composition course, you will likely be using MLA as the primary method of citing sources. However, since many college disciplines require APA citation, it is important to become acquainted with both styles in order to be adequately prepared moving forward.

Before you begin to glance over the format of both citation styles, it is important to note that MLA and APA share similarities as to how they operate, as well as how they are formatted. For instance, both styles have a page, or more, at the end of a paper that list the sources used. The formatting is very similar, as each use what is known as a hanging indent, and the listing of sources are alphabetized on both. Despite their similarities, one of the noticeable differences between the MLA and APA citation section of the paper is the title. In MLA, this section is titled "Works Cited," while in APA, it is referred to as the "References" section.

Another significant similarity is that MLA and APA both use parenthetical in-text citations. A parenthetical citation is relevant source information that appears inside of your paper after you use information from that source by means of a summary, paraphrase, or a quote. Each in-text citation that you have in your paper should have a corresponding source entry in the citation section of your paper. The formatting rules for MLA versus APA parenthetical citations differ. In the following sections, you will explore the differences, and you will see how each citation style has its own way of operating.

MLA Citation: A Brief Overview

The "Works Cited" section of an MLA paper provides a list of sources that are used in a student's paper. In regards to length, this section is usually a page long, but it can be longer, especially if you are writing papers of considerable length. This alphabetized list of sources that uses a hanging indent will appear like the following:

Works Cited

Angelo White, Dana. "The Plant-Based Food Trends We Expect to See in 2021." *Food Network's Healthyeats*, 1 Dec. 2020, www.foodnetwork.com/healthyeats/news/plant-based-trends-2021.

Dead Kennedys. "Soup is Good Food." *Frankenchrist*, Alternative Tentacles Records, 1985.

"East Coast's Finest." *Beat Bobby Flay*, season 4, episode 8, *Food Network*, 23 April 2015. *foodnetwork.com*, www.imdb.com/title/tt4612324/.

Guarnschelli, Alex. *Old-School Comfort Food: The Way I Learned to Cook*. Clarkson Potter, 2013.

Otake, Keiko and Kenji Kato. "Subjective Happiness and Emotional Responsiveness to Food Stimuli." *Journal of Happiness Studies*, vol. 18, 2017, pp. 691-708. EBSCOhost, doi.org/10.1007/s10902-016-9747-8.

So, how do you set up a source in the MLA Works Cited? To assemble your documented source correctly, you must plug in the information that you have using the following nine components:

The 9 Components & Punctuations	The Works Cited Format
1. Author's Last Name, First Name. 2. Title of the Source. 3. Title of the Container, 4. Contributors, 5. Version, 6. Number, 7. Publisher, 8. Publication Date, 9. Location.	Author's Last Name, First Name. Title of the Source. Title of the Container, Contributors, Version, Number, Publisher, Publication Date, Location.

While most of the nine entries are self-explanatory (a contributor, for example, is an individual beside the primary authors or editors, such as an illustrator or translator, who contributed to the source in a way that is germane to your essay), it is important to know what the container is and how it works. The container, as the name suggests, is the larger work that contains the source. For instance, when an article is contained in a magazine, the article would be the source and the magazine would be the container. Another matter that needs explanation is the absence of certain components. In other words, just because you find a source does not mean it will have information to complete the "Version" and "Number" components. Therefore, you should simply ignore them and only fill out the information that you do have. The following example demonstrates how this works:

The 9 Components & Punctuations

The Works Cited Format

1. Smith, John.
2. "My Life."
3. *Imaginary Magazine,*
4. Contributors,
5. Version,
6. Vol. 50, no. 5,
7. Publisher,
8. Winter 2021,
9. pp. 34-42.

Smith, John. "My Life." *Imaginary Magazine,* vol. 50, no. 5, Winter 2021, pp. 34-42.

In the example, the information in green is the information that you have available from a source while the information in red is information that you do not have available. Notice that the available information is formatted for the Works Cited on the right-hand side of the image with the unavailable information (the contributors, version, and publisher) omitted.

The MLA in-text citations are the final ingredient to properly citing sources. As stated earlier, they appear within the text of your paper (author or authors and page number in parentheses) and relate the information used in your paper back to the sources documented in the Works Cited. In order to see how MLA in-text citations function, look at the previous example:

Smith, John. "My Life." *Imaginary Magazine*, vol. 50, no. 5, Winter 2021, pp. 34-42.

With this example in place, it is now important to point out that MLA in-text citations can function by either being included in the prose of your paper or in parentheses. The following examples demonstrate how this works:

Prose Citation

John Smith argues that the key to a happy life is "good friends" (35).

Parenthetical Citation

It has been argued that the key to a happy life is good friends (Smith 35).

As you may have noticed, MLA in-text citations begin with the first of the nine components listed in any documented source. In the Smith example, the word "Smith" is the first component listed for that documented sources. Therefore, the word "Smith" is the bridge word that connects the information inside of the paper to its proper source in the Works Cited. However, what happens when you do not have an author? What if you only have an article title? Take a look at this next sample source that appears on a Works Cited:

"My Life." Imaginary Magazine, vol. 50, no. 5, Winter 2021, pp. 34-42.

This documented source is pretty much the same as the previous example, but you will notice that no author is listed. This documented source begins with the article title. In order to provide a proper in-text citation for this listed source, you would use the first few words of the article title rather than the author's last name. Take a look at the following examples:

Prose Citation: The article "My Life" argues that the key to a happy life is "good friends" (35).

Parenthetical Citation: It has been argued that the key to a happy life is good friends ("My Life" 35).

Because the altered example source in the Works Cited now begins with the article title "My Life" rather than Smith, the in-text citations must also now be altered to correspond to the documented source in the Works Cited. However, one important question remains: why are some titles italicized while others have quotation marks around them? What is the rule, or standard for properly marking titles in MLA? Simply put, major titles (such as the titles of books, newspapers, and magazines) are italicized while the titles of smaller works (such as poems, newspaper articles, and magazine articles) have quotation marks around them.

APA Citation: A Brief Overview

Like MLA, the "References" section in an APA paper provides a list of sources that students use in their papers. Again, like MLA, the length of this citation section is usually a page long, but it can be longer. Upon first glance, an APA "References" section may look exactly like an MLA "Works Cited" section, since it is alphabetized and has hanging indents. However, when you look closely, you will see many differences. Take a look at the following sample "References" page:

References

Angelo White, D. (2020, December 1). The plant-based food trends we expect to see in 2021. *Food Network's healthyeats*. https://www.foodnetwork.com/healthyeats/news/plant-based-trends-2021

Bartley, M. (Director). (2015). East coast's finest. (Series 4, Episode 8). *Beat Bobby Flay*. Embassy Row and Rock Shrimp Productions. https://www.imdb.com/title/tt4612324/

Guarnschelli, A. (2013). *Old-School comfort food: The way I learned to cook.* Clarkson Potter.

Otake, K & Kato, K. (2017). Subjective happiness and emotional responsiveness to food stimuli. *Journal of Happiness Studies*, 6, 691-708. https://doi.org/10.1007/s10902-016-9747-8

Ray, E.B, Flouride, K., Peligro, D.H., & Biafra, J. (1985). Soup is good food [Song recorded by Dead Kennedys]. On *Frankenchrist*. Alternative Tentacles Records.

To assemble your documented source correctly in the Reference section, you must plug in the information that you have using the following four components:

1. Author or Editor (Who?)

Use the author's last name followed by a comma and then the author's first initials.

Ex: Smith, J.

If you have an editor, include the abbreviation "Ed." in parentheses after the name.

Ex: Smith, J. (Ed.)

Join two names with a comma and an ampersand (&).

Ex: Smith, J. P., & Smith J. A.

2. Date (When?)

Provide the year the work was copyrighted or published in parentheses.

Ex: (2021).

If you have a multivolume work published over more than a single year, put the span of years in parentheses.

Ex: (2015–2021).

If no year of publication is provided, write "n.d." (meaning "no date") in parentheses.

Ex: (n.d.).

3. Title (What?)

For Books…

- Italicize book titles.

- Capitalize only the first word, the first word after a colon, and proper nouns.

- Close with a period.

For Periodicals…

- Do not use quotation marks.

- Capitalize only the first word of the title, the first word of the subtitle, and proper nouns.

For Internet Sources…

- Website titles should be treated like any book title.

- Webpages and internet articles should be treated like any other article title.

4. Source (Where?)

Publication Information…

- List the city name followed by a comma and the state abbreviation.

- No abbreviations allowed in the publisher's name.

Journal Title…

- Italicize journal titles.

- Capitalize all words except articles and coordinating conjunctions (they are only capitalized if they are the first word of the title or subtitle).

Volume, Issue, and Page Numbers…

- Italicize the volume number followed by the issue number inside of parentheses.

- Include the page or page range where the title is located, if applicable.

DOI or URL…

- If an article has a digital object Identifier (DOI), then write "DOI" followed by a colon with the DOI afterward with no period at the end.

- URL must be written exactly as it appears in the browser.

Recall the John Smith example from the previous MLA section of this chapter. When you document the Smith example using the four APA components, you will notice that it is somewhat different than that of its MLA counterpart. Take a look at the following image:

The 4 Components & Punctuations	The Reference Format
1. Smith, J. 2. (2021) 3. My life. 4. *Imaginary Magazine, 50*(5), 34-42.	Smith, J. (2021). My life. *Imaginary Magazine, 50*(5), 34-42.

The APA in-text citations serve the exact same purpose as MLA in-text citations. In fact, APA in-text citations can also be included in the sentence itself (which is known as a narrative citation) or as a parenthetical citation at the end of a sentence, just like MLA. Despite this similarity, the APA format of the narrative and parenthetical citations are different than those of their counterpart as the following examples show:

Narrative Citation

John Smith (2021) argues that the key to a happy life is "good friends."

Parenthetical Citation

It has been argued that the key to a happy life is good friends (Smith, 2021).

You will notice that the year in parentheses immediately follows the author's name in the APA narrative citation. In the parenthetical citation at the end of the sentence, you include the author's last name, followed by a comma, and then the year. However, you need to make sure that you properly use the in-text citations, and if you recall, the John Smith example had page numbers included in the documented source. Therefore, you will need to add the page number(s) to the in-text citation. To do so, you will need to add another comma after the date, write "p." for page and then the number. The in-text citation will then appear like one of the following examples:

Narrative Citation

John Smith (2021) argues that the key to a happy life is "good friends" (p.40).

Parenthetical Citation

It has been argued that the key to a happy life is good friends (Smith, 2021, p.40).

Now that you have received some initial information on MLA and APA, you might be thinking, "Why do I have to cite sources in my papers?" Well, the answer is simple: you do not want to plagiarize your paper. Plagiarism is a serious, egregious offense and occurs when a writer takes information from a source and declares it as his or her own. In other words, it is stealing.

Political Cartoons

Make no mistake about it: political cartoons are arguments. While the cartoonist presents graphics and caricatures that may be exaggerated, ironic, satiric, and often downright funny, the message of cartoon, most often, is no laughing matter. The issue often resonates as something serious, or at least something current that demands our immediate consideration and attention. The subject matter of the cartoon is usually timely, making you pause and contemplate current societal and political issues that, from the cartoonist's perspective, you may have overlooked.

The cartoonist *assumes* something about you—that you know something about, or are at least familiar with, the characters and issue the cartoonist presents. You recognize the caricature of the president, a senator, an actor; you know their ideologies and platforms; you discern the policy and position differences between Democrats and Republicans on major issues such as gun control, abortion, immigration, and taxation. What the cartoonist assumes about you is unstated. You recognize that a visual distortion, such as a character's growing or enlarged nose, suggests that he is a liar. You recognize symbols. Uncle Sam personifies the government of the United States. An eagle signifies independence and freedom, a phoenix rebirth and renewal, and a stork, birth (you are familiar with the legend that storks deliver babies). You are able to determine the theme, the bite or perspective, of the artist through the visual images and the captions—a few words reinforcing the nonverbal elements of the cartoon and aiding you in interpreting the cartoonist's main point.

When analyzing the content of the cartoon in order to discern the artist's argument, or claim, ask yourself the following questions.

1. What is familiar? What do you recognize? What about the cartoon is unfamiliar, or unexpected? How does the unexpected, the *surprise* of the cartoon, aid in helping you understand the artist's purpose or point of view?

2. What does the cartoonist *assume* that you know? What values or beliefs does he or she believe you share? What must you be aware of, what must you already know, in order to comprehend the cartoonist's full message?

3. What is the *mood* or *tone* of the cartoon? What is exaggerated, ironic, satirical, contradictory, symbolic, humorous, and/or serious? In what ways does the mood contribute to the meaning?

4. What is the cartoonist's *claim*, or point of view?

5. What textual and visual *evidence* does the cartoonist use to support this claim? Look at the setting, the characters, the captions, and thought bubbles.

Study Steve Kelley's cartoon (Figure 11.1) which appeared in the January 27, 2019 issue of the *Pittsburgh Post-Gazette*, as well as the analysis that follows.

Figure 11.1

1. What may be familiar to you is a teenage boy reprimanded by an older woman for wearing a Make America Great Again (MAGA) hat. You may also recognize the young man, and the woman's hat, from multiple social media reports concerning recent demonstrations and rallies. Note your initial impression of what you found surprising or ironic.

2. Kelley, the cartoonist, assumes that you are familiar with the red MAGA hat, a symbol of President Trump's campaign and agenda. Even though the phrase "Make America Great Again" had been used earlier by politicians such as Ronald Reagan and Bill Clinton, Trump trademarked the phrase in 2012 and used it during his presidential campaign. The results have been divisive. For some, the hat symbolizes patriotism, pride, hope, and strength—a return to the days, to the decades, when America thrived in power, influence, innovation, and wealth. For others, however, separated from such power and wealth, the MAGA hat symbolizes privilege and polarization. Although America may have been, or still is, great to many, others, including minorities, voice that they have not shared equal treatment, wealth, opportunity, and power. Thus, for the woman pointing her finger at the teenager, the hat is "offensive."

   Kelly also assumes that you are familiar with the story of MAGA hat attired teenager Nick Sandmann, the Kentucky Covington Catholic student involved in a "stare-down" confrontation with Nathan Phillips, a Native American activist, during group demonstrations near the Lincoln Memorial in Washington, DC. The cartoon also assumes that you are aware of, or that you are able to recognize, the symbolism of the woman's hat, the "Pussyhat," which, for some, makes a stout, visual statement for unification for women's rights, while, for others, in its representation of female genitalia, in color and shape, is offensive, even vulgar.

3. The mood of the cartoon is confrontational. The woman points her finger as she approaches the teenager. For her, the hat itself is antagonistic, confrontational. She leans towards him; he leans back. Notice his eye. He looks at the hat. What is the irony here? What is the tone?

4. Through the biting irony, and in begging the question to his audience as to which hat is more "offensive," Kelley's point of view, or claim, becomes readily apparent.

5. The evidence in the cartoon includes the divisive MAGA hat, the words in the speech balloon, and the Pussyhat. The ironic notion that the woman preoccupied with approaching the teenager about his "offensive" hat is unaware of reactions of others to her own hat contributes to the evidence and theme of the cartoon.

In-Class Activity

Locate the claim in Steve Kelley's February 28, 2021 *Pittsburgh Post-Gazette* cartoon (Figure 11.2) by analyzing the cartoon's setting, tone, characters, assumptions, and visual evidence. What is Kelley's argument or point of view? How do you know?

Figure 11.2

Editorial Cartoon Assignments

1. Make a copy of an editorial or political cartoon and thoroughly analyze it using by applying the above critiquing principles.

2. Create your own editorial or political cartoon. What current issue stands out for you that you want to make fun of, expose, show the irony, or call for change? Start with an issue that you feel strongly about, reflect upon your assumptions concerning what the audience will know about the topic, and then create a visual argument revealing your point of view. Consider including a thematic or visual twist or surprise that will lead your audience to the joke or core of the issue and your argument.

3. Find two or three cartoons in current newspapers and magazines with different arguments or points of view that address the same issue. Which cartoon, for you, is most persuasive? Why? When answering this question, consider not only the effectiveness of the visual evidence and cleverness of the cartoon but also your own prior bias or perspective about the issue.

The Op-Ed, Editorial, and Letter to the Editor

Opinions are ubiquitous. When you are on a bus, in a grocery store line, or in a barber's chair, it is rare not to hear the opinions of others, and often frustrating, if the opinion you hear is not your own, to be stuck on that bus or in that line or swiveling chair for a while. While you can often refine your own opinions by listening to those of others, at times you feel compelled to share your own opinions and help to "refine" those of others. Op-ed pieces, editorials, and letters to the editors are common channels for writers to voice their point of view and be heard. Op-ed, which stands for "opposite the editorial page," are opinion pieces written by critics not affiliated with the newspaper or magazine in which the article appears. Members of a newspaper or magazine's editorial board write editorials. Readers or subscribers of a newspaper or magazine write letters to the editor. In essence, op-eds, editorials, and letters to the editor have one thing in common: they are arguments, with claims that are most often loud and clear.

Op-eds, editorials, and letters to the editors are persuasive pieces intended to encourage critical analysis, sway public opinion, and incite action concerning a current problem or issue. Sometimes they simply explain the stated reasoning behind an important or controversial act, and then justify or decry the action taken. While op-eds, editorials, and letters to the editor may first look like regular news stories in their openings by including the vital journalistic questions of who, what, when, where, and why, as well as by carefully and objectively clarifying multifaceted issues for the lay reader, ultimately, they are not objective. Good op-eds, editorials, and letters to the editor focus on the issue rather than on an *ad hominem*, recognize the merits and expose the weaknesses in the opposing points of view, and offer constructive solutions to problems.

Compare and Contrast Writing Exercise: The Opinion Piece

Read Ben Shapiro's "Sex Before Marriage Won't Make You Happy" (*Newsweek*, October 26, 2018, https://www.newsweek.com/ben-shapiro-sex-marriage-wont-make-you-happy-opinion-1188744) and Bromleigh McCleneghan's "Sex and the Single Christian: Why Celibacy Isn't the Only Option" (*The Washington Post*, August 22, 2016, https://www.washingtonpost.com/news/acts-of-faith/wp/2016/08/22/sex-and-the-single-christian-why-celibacy-isnt-the-only-option/). Which point of view, for you, is more persuasive? Use critical analysis and textual evidence to explain why.

The Research Paper: The Argument Synthesis

The purpose of the argument synthesis is to research and find evidence to support your point of view. Think of your argument thesis as your claim that you will back and attempt to prove through appeals to logic, emotion, and sources. Your job when writing an argument is to persuade. By providing and combining (synthesizing) information from multiple sources, you strategically build evidence that "proves" your opening claim.

Note that others may be able to use the same sources you use, or other sources, to build a strong counterclaim. Remember claims are not facts; claims are proposals or points of view for which sensible individuals may disagree. Your job is to support your claim, include the merits of the counterclaim, and then persuade your audience as to why you believe your perspective is stronger than that of the counterargument. Reasonable individuals can easily find merit in opposing points of view. Urgent persuasion, through thorough, logical appeals and support, can advance your claim over that of your challenger.

First-year composition students Joe McKernan and Hollie Imperato each synthesize reasonable arguments concerning the gender wage gap. Be prepared to discuss how, with each, you are persuaded to agree.

The Myth of the Gender Wage Gap

Joe McKernan

In 2014, the Shriver Report declared that women only earn seventy-seven cents for every dollar earned by men ("A Woman's Nation"). For gender wage gap activists, this statistic is the basis to argue that the cause is gender discrimination and that women are paid less for the same job and equal work. A large number of people accept this claim as truth, but many people question it and demand evidence for this claim. To get to the truth, it is necessary to understand what this statistic measures and what it does not. This statistic is calculated by dividing the median earnings of all women working full time by the median earnings of all men working full time, in every job. It does not take into account any variables that affect the earnings of a worker, such as the choice of career, education, hours worked per week, and years worked in the labor force without significant time off ("There Is No"). Once those variables are included in the study of any gender wage gap, the gap shrinks to almost zero. The wage gap in the United States does not exist because of discrimination or unfair employment practices; it exists because women and men make different choices for their lives.

GENDER GAP

© TarikVision/Shutterstock.com

Men and women are not exactly alike and often desire different things. A look at college majors provides a window into why men and women choose different professions. When a student applies to college, he or she chooses what to learn and what career to pursue. Some majors appeal more to men and others more to women. Men tend to choose majors in science, technology, engineering, and mathematics, while women tend to choose majors in health care, education, and service.

Certain majors lead to jobs that pay higher salaries than others. Georgetown University studied and listed the five college majors that result in the highest salaries and the five college majors with the lowest salaries. The University also listed the percent of men and women in these majors. The top five best paying college majors are petroleum engineering which is 87% male; pharmaceutical sciences which is 52% female; mathematics and computer science which is 67% male; aerospace engineering which is 88% male; and chemical engineering which is 72% male. Four of the top five paying college majors are male dominated majors. Pharmaceutical sciences is the only major comprised of more women than men, and it is only by a slim margin.

The list of the five worst paying college majors according to the Georgetown University study are counseling and psychology which is 74% female; early childhood education which is 97% female; theology and religious vocations which is 66% male; human services and community organization which is 81% female; and social work which is 88% female. Women comprise the majority in four of the top five worst paying majors by a large margin. These statistics show that when given the opportunity to choose a major to study in college, women choose lower paying majors than men (Carnevale et al. 15).

Once you control for choice of education and career, the next question is whether or not women and men with the same education and jobs make the same amount of money. In order to have an honest discussion of this issue, one must consider not only educational level and job requirements, but the amount of hours worked and any significant time out of the career market. According to a 2015 study of full-time employees by the US Bureau of Labor Statistics, men worked 8.2 hours per day while women worked 7.8 hours per day (Agness). In addition, women take off significant time during childrearing years to stay home and provide care for their children and families. Often these same women return to their career, but have lost years of experience that make their value to an employer less than an employee who continually worked, produced, and gained valuable job experience. A comprehensive 2009 study by the US Department of Labor evaluated more than 50 peer-reviewed studies and found that the gender wage gap could almost entirely be due to the choices made by men and women ("There Is No").

An example often used by wage gap activists is that male nurses make 18% more money than female nurses. However, once you account for the factors that men in nursing choose higher paying specialties, work longer hours, and take jobs in cities which pay higher salaries, you find out, as Professor Linda Aiken of the University of Pennsylvania notes, "…career choices and educational differences explain most, if not all, the gender gap in nursing" ("There Is No").

Proponents of the wage gap myth often argue that women choose those career paths because of society's stereotypes that force women out of higher paying careers. In order to accept that argument, one must believe that women, when asked what they want to pursue as a career, lie. They don't really want to be teachers or nurses and they spend tens of thousands of dollars to pursue a college major for a career they are forced to choose. That position lacks reason because many women choose careers that are male dominant and are very successful (Sommers, "Wage Gap"). Moreover, dangerous and well-paying jobs such as logging, commercial fishing, mining, and truck driving are male dominated jobs. In fact, the rate of fatalities for men at work is ten times great than for women (DeVore). Women simply do not choose high risk jobs and nowhere do the proponents of the wage gap myth complain about the death gap difference between men and women at work.

Gender wage gap activists also argue that additional stereotypes push women into family caretaking roles and force women out of the workforce or into lower paying jobs with more flexibility. This argument fails to consider what women actually want when it comes to choosing how to manage their career and childcare. Research shows that with an at home parent, children do better in school, have less stress, and fewer behavioral problems. A 2014 Pew Research study revealed that 60 percent of Americans believe that it is better for children to have one parent at home. It is likely that many stay-at-home moms agree with this sentiment and are freely choosing to leave their jobs, or work different jobs for lower pay but with more flexibility, to care for their children (Cohn et al.).

Faced with evidence of the incomplete and misleading nature of the gender wage gap statistics, even some wage gap activists are forced to concede that "more than half is due to the differences in the types of occupations and industries in which men and women work. Additionally, about 14 percent is due to the fact that women are more likely to leave the workforce to provide unpaid care to family members" (Holmes and Corley). Having admitted these truths, wage gap proponents now move the goalpost and abandon their statistical arguments in favor of amorphous and non-measurable factors to keep the issue of wage inequality alive. They now argue that unconscious bias is responsible for the remaining gap (Elesesser). In order to remedy this problem, they recommend unconscious bias training at work and government regulations that require reporting of wages and promotions by employers to the government to ensure that women are paid the same wage for the same job (Elesesser). This gives the government the power to punish employers by looking at their employee compensation without knowing anything about the business or any other factors that are important to the employers' decisions of what to pay their employees. It is wage control by the government and would change our market-based economy to a command economy. Another idea advocated by Carmen Sirianni and Cynthia Negrey in *Feminist Economics* is that society should pay working mothers and stay at home mothers a "social wage" to promote equality between the genders. This proposal would create a new government entitlement program requiring taxpayers to pay women a wage above what they earn in a job, or even if they do not work outside the home.

The gender wage gap is a myth. Once factors such as career choice, hours worked, and continuity of employment are accounted for, the gap essentially disappears. This is only logical because if the gender wage gap was really seventy-seven cents to the dollar, why would any employer hire a man for a dollar when that same employer could hire a woman for the same job and equal work for almost twenty-five percent less (Sommers, "The Gender")? The answer is they would not. While many gender wage gap activists continue to rely on this discredited statistic, others have moved beyond arguing about it and instead no longer simply advocate for equal pay for equal work, but for government wage control of businesses, and payment of a social wage to women which is completely unrelated to their employment or lack thereof.

Works Cited

Agness, Karin. "New Report: Men Work Longer Hours Than Women." *Forbes, Forbes Magazine*, 30 June 2016. www.forbes.com/sites/karinagness/2016/06/30/new-report-men-work-longer-hours-than-women/#78cf32f18b4e. According to the 2015 American Time Use Survey by the U.S. Bureau of Labor Statistics.

"A Woman's Nation Pushes Back from the Brink: Facts and Figures." *The Shriver Report*, 12 January 2014, shriverreport.org/a-womans-nation-pushes-back-from-the-brink-facts-and-figures/

Carnevale, A., Strohl, J., Melton, M. 2011. *What is it worth? The economic values of college majors.* Georgetown University Center on Education and the Workforce, Washington, DC. p. 15, cew.georgetown.edu/wp-content/uploads/2014/11/whatsitworth-complete.pdf

Cohn, D'Vera, Livingston, Gretchen, and Wendy Wang. "Stay-at-Home Mothers on the Rise." Project, Pew Research Center's Social & Demographic Trends Project, 6 June 2014, www.pewsocialtrends.org/2014/04/08/after-decades-of-decline-a-rise-in-stay-at-home-mothers/

DeVore, Chuck. "Fatal Employment: Men 10 Times More Likely Than Women To Be Killed At Work." *Forbes, Forbes Magazine,* 19 Dec. 2018, www.forbes.com/sites/chuckdevore/2018/12/19/fatal-employment-men-10-times-more-likely-than-women-to-be-killed-at-work/

Elsesser, Kim. "Unequal Pay, Unconscious Bias, And What To Do About It." *Forbes, Forbes Magazine*, 10 Apr. 2018, www.forbes.com/sites/kimelsesser/2018/04/10/unequal-pay-unconscious-bias-and-what-to-do-about-it/#6fb6594f600e

Holmes, Kaitlin, and Danielle Corley. "The Top 10 Facts about the Gender Wage Gap." Center for American Progress, 12 April 2016. www.americanprogress.org/issues/women/reports/2016/04/12/135260/the-top-10-facts-about-the-gender-wage-gap/

Sirianni, Carmen, and Cynthia Negrey. "Working Time as Gendered Time, by Carmen Sirianni; Cynthia Negrey." *51st Annual Transportation Research Forum, Arlington, Virginia, March 11-13, 2010*, Transportation Research Forum, 1 January 1970. ideas.repec.org/a/taf/femeco/v6y2000i1p59-76.html

Sommers, Christina Hoff. "The Gender Wage Gap Myth and 5 Other Feminist Fantasies." *Time*, 2 September 2014. time.com/3222543/wage-pay-gap-myth-feminism/

Sommers, Christina Hoff. "Wage Gap Myth Exposed -- By Feminists." *The Huffington Post*, 23 January 2014. www.huffingtonpost.com/christina-hoff-sommers/wage-gap_b_2073804.html

"There Is No Gender Wage Gap." PragerU. YouTube, YouTube, 6 March 2017. www.youtube.com/watch?v=QcDrE5YvqTs

The Wage Gap: A Penalty of Having a Child

Hollie Imperato

The wage gap between men and women doing the same job is an issue present in every country on the planet. This may seem like a broad claim, but even Iceland, which is ranked number one in the world for wage equality, has a 4.5% wage gap (Wood). Much of the time, the wage gap is associated with sexism. If women are just as smart, capable and worthy as men, it is a logical assumption to assume that sexism must be behind the wage gap. In the United States, there are laws against gender discrimination in the workplace and regulations in place to prevent sexism. However, the United States, the land of opportunity, lands 50th in the Global Gender Gap Report. If these laws and regulations are in place, then how are women in the United States paid about 75 cents for every dollar a man makes? Though the issue of sexism is involved in the wage gap of the United States, it is not the main factor; a woman's decision to have a child is the main reason that the wage gap exists.

With the United States becoming increasingly more modern, women's rights are certainly improving. In the 1950's, discriminatory pay for women was legal, and the general opinion about women was that they were less intelligent, unable to hold powerful positions, and meant to raise children (Posner). Thankfully, much of these opinions have changed in the 21st century. However, it is not just this sexist opinion that creates the wage gap; it is the missed opportunities the woman experiences due to the obligation of child care. Henrik Kleven, an economist at Princeton University, conducted research concerning the career trajectories between men and women with and without children. He found that young men and women without children start out with almost the same income trajectory with little to no gap in wage. However, as soon as a woman births her first child, she experiences an immediate drop in gross earnings of almost 30%, whereas men's salaries are unaffected (Kleven et al.). This is due to several factors, but mostly to the fact that maternity leave is typically offered to women and rarely to men. This requires women to take an unpaid leave from her job, missing opportunities for promotions and experience.

Along with childbirth come maternity and paternity leaves which heavily influence the issue of the wage gap. In the United States, most maternity leave is unpaid and the Family Medical Leave Act can only protect certain employee positions for up to twelve weeks. Maternity leave can differ between employers, but men rarely get the opportunity of paternity leave and when they do, only 25% of men get more than a week off ("Paternity

Leave"). Without a reasonable paternity leave, the mother has few options and has to take the maternity leave in order to care for the child. A solution to this can be observed in Iceland, the country with the lowest wage gap in the world. Iceland instituted the Act on Maternity/Paternity Leave, which enforced 6-month paid maternity *and* paternity leaves that are completely obligatory (Posner). In doing this, it changes the structure of society because men and women alike expect to take a six month leave to take care of their child. This not only significantly

alters society and how it views childcare, but it also levels employment for men and women. With this law, an employer can expect that both female and male candidates for a job will take the same leave, significantly decreasing gender discrimination. Before instituting this law in 2004, Icelandic women made 81 cents to the dollar; in 2018, women made 90 cents to the dollar while the American wage gap remained constant (Posner). This clearly shows that the wage gap is more of a motherhood penalty rather than an issue of sexism.

Now that a successful national model has been examined, we can examine similar efforts within the United States. Though the United States is the only developed country in the world that does not offer any paid parental leave, California and Rhode Island both have state-mandated maternity and paternity paid leaves in place that prove that the wage gap is heavily reliant on women having children (Livingston and Thomas). As a result of having the strongest childcare leave and equal pay laws in the country, California is the state with the lowest wage gap at 11%; Rhode Island isn't far behind with very similar paid leave laws with a 16% wage gap as compared to the national 25% gap (Nielsen). If these laws were instituted at the national level, the average wage gap between men and women would decrease dramatically as it did in California and Rhode Island.

However, I am aware that there are many factors that influence the wage gap and that the causes of the wage gap are widely discussed. Many people, at first glance, view the wage gap as a result of discrimination against women. It is true that historically, women have been treated as the lesser sex compared to men. Due to this, the stigma of a woman being a caretaker itself is a sexist view and has not changed in many years. Less than 20% of Americans feel that women should work full time as a new mother, whereas 70% of Americans feel that new fathers should work full time (Posner). This is a huge problem in American culture. Women are seen as the softer, more caring and loving sex and are often expected to have the responsibility of caring for children. Due to this, the new mother could work fewer hours, or not at all, resulting in the wage gap.

Along with this issue, female intelligence has been belittled in the past as well. Women have been discouraged to participate in STEM majors that are traditionally male dominated and include higher wages due to the sexist idea that women are less capable. According to the U.S. Department of Commerce, females occupy less than 25% of STEM jobs, creating a vast disparity in income and equality between men and women (Beede et al. 1). It is often argued that this difference in employment as a result of sexism is the main culprit of the wage gap because men have more opportunities to make more money with higher paying jobs.

In light of these counterarguments, I would like to point out that women have made more progress than these arguments are giving credit for. Yes, in the past women have been discouraged from STEM fields because they were not viewed as smart enough for the curriculum. However, there has been a huge push for women in STEM recently, with programs being implemented in K-12 schools such as National Girls Collaborative Project, Association for Women in Science, and Girls Who Code. Due to these initiatives, research has shown that women in biological sciences have more than doubled between 1993 and 2010, resulting in 48% female occupancy of these jobs, and the rate of women in mathematics has nearly doubled in the same time frame as well ("Has Employment of Women"). We can't blame sexism in STEM jobs for the wage gap because it is no longer relevant, and women are even encouraged to participate in STEM. Additionally, the wage gap can only be fairly evaluated between men and women with the same jobs, so it is not fair to compare a man and a woman with completely different jobs (Kleven et al.).

As for the view of women as caretakers, this indeed is still an issue. However, society is making a stride in the media towards father appreciation. Large companies such as Dove, Swiffer and Pampers have portrayed comfortable caretaking fathers in commercials to promote a father's role as equal to a mother's (Bedera). This has not fully changed the view of mothers, but it is certainly helping. In addition, it was previously stated that men and women have little to no wage gap before having children. So if it was purely sexist reasoning behind the wage gap, wouldn't there be a gap regardless of whether a woman has a child? In regards to the argument that mothers work less, even if the mother returns to her job and works the same hours ten years after the child is born, "the new mother's earnings remain 20% below what she made before childbirth," which strongly suggests that hours worked has little to do with the gap. Having a child, she will always be behind (Kleven et al.).

Women have come a long way in the workplace. More and more women are attending college and getting degrees in STEM majors and are making important and respected contributions to our society. However, the wage gap does still exist, especially for mothers in the United States. With the current maternity leaves and views on motherhood, a female is much more likely to take time off of work to raise children. This is not a result of sexism or men being unwilling to do the same; rather, it is an issue of what is available in our country and the results of women having little choice but to take unpaid time off of work. The wage gap is a motherhood penalty not just because of maternity leave; when there is a school meeting, a doctor's appointment, or emergency, the mother is more likely to leave work and tend to her child because employers rarely extend this flexibility to men. A woman with the same job as a man, with the same experience and education, *without* children makes 96 cents to the dollar (Posner). If this is true, then it is clear the wage gap is not just a result of a purely discriminatory society; it is mostly the result of a society that is unsupportive of working mothers.

Works Cited

Bedera, Nichole. "Dads In Advertising." 27 February 2015, psmag.com/economics/dads-in-advertising-are-times-changing

Beede, David , Julian, Tiffany, Langdon, David, McKittrick, George, Khan, Beethika, and Mark Doms. "Women in STEM: A Gender Gap to Innovation." *SSRN Electronic Journal*, August 2011, pp. 1–2. doi:10.2139/ssrn.1964782.

"Has Employment of Women and Minorities in S&E Jobs Increased?" *NSF Award Search: Award#0700410 - International Research Fellowship Program: Regulation of Rhodopsin Photochemistry by Arrestin*, nsf.gov/nsb/sei/edTool/data/workforce-07.html

Kleven, Henrik, Landais, Camille, and Jakob Egholt Sogaard. "Children and Gender Inequality: Evidence from Denmark." *American Economic Journal: Applied Economics*, vol. 11, no. 4, 2019, pp. 181–209. www.nber.org/papers/w24219

Livingston, Gretchen, and Deja Thomas. "Of 41 Countries, Only U.S. Lacks Paid Parental Leave." *Pew Research Center*, Pew Research Center, 26 September 2016. www.pewresearch.org/fact-tank/2016/09/26/u-s-lacks-mandated-paid-parental-leave/

Nielsen, Kate. "The Gender Pay Gap by State: An Interactive Map." *AAUW: Empowering Women Since 1881*, 2019. https://ww3.aauw.org/resource/gender-pay-gap-by-state-and-congressional-district/

"Paternity Leave in the U.S. Leaves a Lot of Gaps." *Online Human Resources Management Degree - Employment Law at Tulane*, 14 February 2018. employment.law.tulane.edu/blog/paternity-leave-for-fathers

Posner, Joe. *Explained: Why Women Are Paid Less. Netflix*, Vox Media , 2018. www.netflix.com/watch/80243768?trackId=200257859

"The Global Gender Gap Report." *World Economic Forum*, 17 December 2018. www3.weforum.org/docs/WEF_GGGR_2018.pdf

Wood, Johnny. "These 4 Nordic Countries Hold the Secret to Gender Equality." *World Economic Forum*, 18 December 2018. www.weforum.org/agenda/2018/12/nordic-countries-women-equality-gender-pay-gap-2018/

Assignments

1. Select a letter to the editor in a newspaper and write a rebuttal letter arguing against the points made by the writer.

2. Select current issues of two magazines written for different specific, or targeted, audiences. Imagine composing an argumentative essay for each. In what ways might your audience's views, values, priorities, and interests differ? What are the differences in your audience's ages, affiliations, social and economic status, and level of education? How might your use of persuasive appeals vary due to the audience demographic?

3. Compose an argument claim. After you have decided on your point of view, first find evidence for the counterclaim and write a thorough counterargument before you consider evidence for your argument, and ways to dilute or overcome the strong points made in the counterargument. If you find that the counterargument is extremely weak, do you have an arguable claim, or a claim that needs to be addressed? If the counterargument is quite strong, might it be stronger than your argument?

4. Write a thoroughly researched essay in which you offer or advance a proposal.

5. Write a well-supported essay in which you advance your position on a topic while including an objective, balanced counterargument.

CPSIA information can be obtained
at www.ICGtesting.com
Printed in the USA
LVHW051140060821
694544LV00001B/1